Book by
George Furth

Music and Lyrics by
Stephen Sondheim

NICK HERN BOOKS

London

www.nickhernbooks.co.uk

A Nick Hern Book

This edition of *Company* first published in Great Britain as a paperback original in 2019 by Nick Hern Books Limited, The Glasshouse, 49a Goldhawk Road, London W12 8QP, by special arrangement with Theatre Communications Group, Inc., New York

Cover photograph of Rosalie Craig as Bobbie by Dan Kennedy
Cover artwork by AKA

Designed and typeset by Nick Hern Books, London
Printed in the UK by Mimeo Ltd, Huntingdon, Cambridgeshire PE29 6XX

A CIP catalogue record for this book is available from the British Library

ISBN 978 1 84842 835 5

'Everything's different, nothing's changed…'
David Benedict

In 1962, writer Helen Gurley Brown surprised America. Within three weeks of publication, *Sex and the Single Girl*, her non-fiction guide for young women seeking commitment-free independence, had sold over two million copies and instantly began determining a generation's views on marriage. But if bookshops were happy selling something sociologically new, life was different on Broadway. In musicals, a traditionally family-friendly art form, sexual politics were abidingly conservative. The mindset finally began to crack in April 1968 with the uptown transfer of the downtown, counter-culture, let-it-all-hang-out hit *Hair: The American Tribal Love-Rock Musical*, but that was a maverick one-off. The real shift came exactly two years later with the first of six consecutive, groundbreaking musicals that Stephen Sondheim created with director Hal Prince over just eleven years.

Company didn't just abandon the stereotypical 'boy gets girl' content of the then typical Broadway musical, it pivoted around a boy who isn't even looking for a girl. Putting the man into Manhattan, Bobby was seeing not one but three girls: Marta, April and Kathy. But on the occasion of his thirty-fifth birthday, and facing down a slew of well-intentioned birthday messages and a threatened surprise party from 'These good and crazy people, my married friends', he finds himself taking stock of his life: Where is he? Where might he be heading? Is commitment a dirty word? Should he be thinking about… marriage?

The idea sprang from eleven one-act plays by actor-turned-playwright George Furth, all of which featured couples in relationships seen from the angle of a succession of single outsiders. When a production of seven of them fell through, Sondheim suggested Furth show them to producer-director Prince who, in turn, suggested they might make a fine springboard for a musical. Having alighted upon the idea of turning all the outsiders into a single person, Bobby, the project took wing.

Strikingly urban, the result was a breath of cool – in every sense – fresh air on Broadway. Putting marriage under a contemporary microscope, it became a fascinating rarity: a musical for adults. The unexpectedly sophisticated bite of its examination of sexual politics didn't just help audiences see the predicaments of its characters, it forced them to examine versions of themselves. The sometimes bracing result did not, therefore, please everyone (musicals were, traditionally, 'supposed' to be predominantly mindless entertainments) and the reviews were mixed – there were both raves and dissenting voices, but its twenty-month run and six Tony Awards including Best Musical were enough to cement the reputations of the senior creative team and, particularly, Sondheim's career as a composer as well as a lyricist.

In the half-century since its 1970 debut, the zesty combination of his first distinctively mature score allied to the perspicacity of Furth's script snappily skewering a number of couples simultaneously celebrating and chafing against their marital state has led to countless productions. And to help keep pace with contemporary attitudes and shifting sexual politics, there have been minor tweaks along the way. The trio 'You Could Drive a Person Crazy' used to contain the lines:

I could understand a person
If it's not a person's bag.
I could understand a person
If a person was a fag.

But by the time of its 1995 Broadway revival, 'fag' had become a powerfully derogatory word so Sondheim rewrote it as:

I could understand a person
If he said to go away.
I could understand a person
If he happened to be gay.

In addition, director Scott Ellis persuaded Sondheim and Furth to return the previously cut song 'Marry Me a Little' to the score to close the first act. There it has remained ever since. Dialogue changes have also happened, not least for Sam Mendes' Donmar Warehouse production in London later that same year. George Furth revived a scene between Bobby and his friend Peter in which the latter hinted at propositioning Bobby into a potential gay relationship. But the biggest change, and the reason for the publication of this fresh version, came via Marianne Elliott, director of the National Theatre's long-running sensations *War Horse* and *The Curious Incident of the Dog in the Night-Time*, both of which made her the first female director to win two Tony Awards.

Sondheim had been a huge admirer of her work since seeing her blazingly theatrical production of Shaw's *Saint Joan* at the National in 2007, while she had long wanted to direct one of his shows. Her production of *West Side Story* almost happened but fell through at the last moment. Then, when she and her producing partner Chris Harper formed their own company, she began thinking about shows with good roles for women. 'Not romantic ingénues,' she says, 'roles for older women because there are so many stories out there which I don't think are being portrayed on stage.' Following her lead, Harper suggested *Company* with Bobby reimagined as a woman.

Her decision to go ahead with the option of changing Bobby to Bobbie was anything but instant. 'I thought: I didn't want to do anything gimmicky or just turn it into a woman's role because "Why not?" This can only happen if it truly works. I wanted it to say something about a woman in this predicament.' Crucially, it should play *as if it had been written for a woman*.

What has happened is not radical surgery. Strikingly little has had to be done to the book and lyrics to accommodate the switch. Yet tweaks and tilts have induced a dramatic shift that revivifies a script that, almost fifty years on, could make some 2018 audiences feel uneasy. In the #MeToo era, the idea of inviting sympathy for a man sleeping with three women, none of whom he's really interested in, plays very differently than to the just-post-Sixties original.

More forcefully, Elliott recognised that while men no longer feel urgency around being thirty-five, for women the stakes are dramatically higher. 'I was very aware when I was in my mid-thirties, and I'm aware of women now at that point, that you get to a place where you think: If I'm going to settle down and start a family I've probably got five years left. Women start worrying about that and questioning what it will mean in terms of their careers. Marrying and having children create something of a crisis point for many, many women. Bobbie is going to be agonising about what she should do. And when she hits her thirty-fifth birthday, she realises she cannot stay in denial any longer. If she wants to settle down, she needs to do something about it – and quick. *Company* absolutely hits that nail on the head.'

Better yet, it's not just Bobbie who fits the regendered scenario. The otherwise plotless show (back then, a massively radical step) entirely consists of the friends lovingly and nosily watching, discussing and fretting about their single friend... and proffering advice. Elliott laughs. 'A thirty-five-year-old woman who is attractive, earns good money, has a great job and is single is clearly going to be the subject of most of her friends' conversations.'

To strengthen the rethink, Elliott switched some of the couples around. The roles/lines spoken by Jenny and David, a friendly couple who smoke dope with Bobbie, have been cleanly swapped. Jenny now has all of David's lines which turns her from being a housewife to being a career-woman. David, meanwhile, speaking what were formerly Jenny's lines, is now a stay-at-home husband looking after the kids. Rare in 1970, this feels completely natural for a contemporary couple. The same lines-swap has also been applied to divorcing couple Susan and Peter.

Similarly, given that in 2018 the group most openly obsessing about the meaning of marriage is gay men, bride-to-be Amy (who sings 'Getting Married Today') and her ultra-reliable fiancé Paul are now a gay couple: Jamie and Paul. Bobby's trio of girlfriends, Marta, Kathy and airhead air-hostess April, are now PJ, Theo and flight-attendant Andy, which, barely changing a word, cunningly refocuses them in terms of present-day male attitudes. Importantly, aside from changes of pronouns, the changes to the text come from previous versions of the script, all written by Furth, who died in 2008.

Two-and-a-half years in conception, the production went ahead not only with Sondheim's permission – initially somewhat sceptical, he applauded the video of Elliott's workshop presentation – but with his active encouragement. Some of the swaps have meant he has provided lyric rewrites. In 'Getting Married Today', the celebrant formerly sang:

Bless this day, pinnacle of life,
Husband joined to wife.

Whereas here it's:

Bless this day, pinnacle of joy,
Boy unites with boy.

He has changed the odd word or phrase about Bobbie to fit the character of a woman, as well supplying neat updates to bring the play into the present. In 'Poor Baby', Sarah used to sing:

Robert ought to have a woman.
Poor baby, all alone,
Evening after evening by the telephone –
We're the only tenderness he's ever known

Whereas in this version Harry sings:

Bobbie ought to have a fella.
Poor baby, all alone,
Nothing much to do except to check her phone.
We're the only closeness that she's really known.

In the grand second-act ensemble number, 'Side by Side', the couples sang:

Never a bother,
Seven times a godfather.

That now becomes:

Pal and pinch-hitter,
Plus a perfect babysitter!

That last lyric points to Elliott's other significant change. In the original production, Donna McKechnie danced a purely orchestral number choreographed by Michael Bennett who would choreograph *Follies* before going on to create and choreograph *A Chorus Line*. That number, 'Tick-Tock', has since been cut from the published text. Elliott has reinstated it as a dream sequence for Bobbie who, in common with many childless women in their mid-thirties, grapples with the idea of motherhood, staged as a vision – or nightmare? – acted out on a dramatic loop by other cast members. What better title could there be for a sequence about a woman's biological clock?

The sequence sets the seal on the reimagining. Throughout the development period and rehearsals, Elliott argued that her approach isn't an aggressive update or a directorial corrective. It's not designed to be definitive, it simply allows audiences to see *Company* from an alternative perspective.

Judging by the rhapsodic reviews the production received on its London premiere, not to mention Sondheim's support for both a cast recording and the publication of this new edition, it's clear that her 'sex and the single girl' vision has proved to be a winner. Individually, the textual shifts are subtle yet the overall effect is seismic. 'It's not "better", it's just different,' she says. 'Doing it this way says something about 2018. I believe truly good writing has the space for very different interpretations.'

David Benedict is a broadcaster and critic. He is currently writing the authorised biography of Stephen Sondheim for Random House (US) and Picador (UK).

Rosalie Craig as Bobbie, surrounded by the company of the 2018 revival of *Company* at the Gielgud Theatre, London
Directed by Marianne Elliott and produced by Elliott & Harper Productions
Production photographs by Brinkhoff/Mögenburg

Gavin Spokes as Harry and Mel Giedroyc as Sarah, watched by Rosalie Craig as Bobbie

Jonathan Bailey as Jamie in 'Getting Married Today'

The company in 'Side by Side by Side'

Patti LuPone as Joanne in 'The Ladies Who Lunch'

Rosalie Craig as Bobbie

Company was first performed at the Alvin Theatre, New York, in April 1970, presented by Harold Prince, in association with Ruth Mitchell. The cast was as follows:

ROBERT	Dean Jones
SARAH	Barbara Barrie
HARRY	Charles Kimbrough
SUSAN	Merle Louise
PETER	John Cunningham
JENNY	Teri Ralston
DAVID	George Coe
AMY	Beth Howland
PAUL	Steve Elmore
JOANNE	Elaine Stritch
LARRY	Charles Braswell
MARTY	Pamela Myers
KATHY	Donna McKechnie
APRIL	Susan Browning

Director	Harold Prince
Set and Projections	Boris Aronson
Costume Designer	D. D. Ryan
Lighting Designer	Robert Ornbo
Musical Director	Harold Hastings
Orchestrations	Jonathan Tunick
Choreographer	Michael Bennett

The revised version of *Company* published here was first
produced by Elliott & Harper Productions and performed at the
Gielgud Theatre, London, on 17 October 2018. The cast, in
order of speaking, was as follows:

JOANNE	Patti LuPone
SUSAN/PRIEST	Daisy Maywood
ANDY	Richard Fleeshman
JAMIE	Jonathan Bailey
PJ	George Blagden
BOBBIE	Rosalie Craig
PETER	Ashley Campbell
SARAH	Mel Giedroyc
HARRY	Gavin Spokes
PAUL	Alex Gaumond
DAVID	Richard Henders
JENNY	Jennifer Saayeng
LARRY	Ben Lewis
THEO	Matthew Seadon-Young

Understudies

BOBBIE	Jennifer Saayeng
ANDY/PJ/THEO	Michael Colbourne
JOANNE/SARAH	Francesca Ellis
PAUL/PETER/ JAMIE	Ewan Gillies
DAVID/HARRY/ LARRY	Grant Neal
JENNY/SUSAN	Jaimie Pruden

Other characters played by members of the company

Director	Marianne Elliott
Choreographer	Liam Steel
Musical Supervisor and Conductor	Joel Fram
Designer	Bunny Christie
Lighting Designer	Neil Austin
Sound Designer	Ian Dickinson for Autograph Sound
Illusions	Chris Fisher
Hair, Wigs and Make-Up Designer	Campbell Young Associates
Orchestrator	David Cullen
Dance Arrangements	Sam Davis
Additional Vocal Arrangements	Joel Fram
Casting Directors	Alastair Coomer CDG and Charlotte Sutton CDG
Fight Directors	Rachel Bown-Williams and Ruth Cooper-Brown for RC-ANNIE
Voice and Dialect Coach	Charmian Hoare
Associate Director	Miranda Cromwell
Assistant Choreographer	Simone Sault
Dramaturg	Nick Sidi
Researcher	Katy Rudd

A Note on this Edition

This is the script from the 2018 West End production of *Company* produced by Elliott & Harper Productions and directed by Marianne Elliott.

In this edition, some of the genders are swapped. Additional lines of dialogue have been sourced from other George Furth scripts for the piece.

Song lyrics are indicated within the text by indenting the lyrics one line below the character name.

Bobbie is the only member of the company who doesn't double. The other thirteen members of the company each has a particular character to play as well as doubling in the company.

There is no dancing or singing ensemble as such.

The narrative is conveyed in a stream of consciousness, and time moves both backwards and forwards, encompassing the past, present and future.

Characters

BOBBIE

SARAH
HARRY

SUSAN
PETER

JENNY
DAVID

JAMIE
PAUL

JOANNE
LARRY

PJ
THEO
ANDY

16

Musical Numbers

ACT ONE

Scene One

BOBBIE*'s empty apartment.* BOBBIE *enters with a helium balloon that reads '35'. She listens to voice messages on her phone.*

JOANNE (*voice-over*). Hi, this is a dirty phone call. Larry and I are going to be in the country so we'll miss any birthday celebrations. Anyway, you're thirty-five. Who wants to celebrate being that old? Well, I only hope I look as good as you when *I'm* your age.

Sound of hang-up. A beep sound, then:

SUSAN (*voice-over, possibly with children in the background*). Hi, Bobbie. It's Susan. Get those guys out of your bed and pick up the phone, will you? I am so envious I can't even talk. Call me.

Sound of hang-up. A beep sound, then:

ANDY (*voice-over*). Hi, Bobbie, it's Andy. (*Pause.*) Oh. I forgot what I was going to say.

Sound of hang-up. A beep sound, then:

JAMIE (*voice-over*). Hi there, it's Jamie. I just called to say that if I'm late for the party tonight please tell Paul that I'm running – oh, wait, you're not supposed to know that there's a – (*Panic, as he tries to save himself.*) Judy? Judy? Oh, goodness, I'm afraid I dialled a wrong number. Sorry. Just ignore this call. (*Speaking to someone else in the distance as he's hanging up.*) Oh God, you're never going to believe what I just did…

Sound of a hang-up. A beep sound, then:

PJ (*voice-over*). Yo, Bob. It's PJ. Long time, no hear. Listen, just to let you know I've had the all-clear from the doctor. We're all good. So… feel free to return my calls, huh?

BOBBIE *changes her voicemail greeting.*

BOBBIE. Hi, this is Bobbie. Yes, today's my birthday. And yes, you may leave a message about how happy you are that I'm turning thirty-five. And whatever you're calling about, my answer is yes.

She hangs up; pours a drink; a series of ghostly offstage individual voices intoning 'Bobbie'; the voices increase in volume as the five married COUPLES *enter from various parts of the stage. They carry wrapped presents and sing and speak without emotion.*

SUSAN *and* JENNY.
    Bobbie, Bobbie,
    Ba ba ba ba ba ba ba ba...
    Bobbie...

HARRY, THEO *and* DAVID *(overlapping)*.
    Bobbie, Bobbie,
    Ba ba ba ba ba ba ba ba...

ANDY, PAUL *and* PJ *(overlapping)*.
    Bobbie, Bobbie,
    Ba ba ba ba ba ba ba ba...

JOANNE, LARRY, JAMIE *and* PETER *(overlapping)*.
    Bobbie, Bobbie,
    Ba ba ba ba ba ba ba ba...

SARAH *(overlapping)*.
    Bobbie, Bobbie...

ALL.
    Ba ba ba ba ba ba ba ba...
    Bobbie...

BOBBIE. My birthday. It's my birthday. Do you know you had me scared to death? I was just about to run out. I was. I mean, I didn't know – I mean, what kind of friends would surprise you on your thirty-fifth birthday? *(Pause.)* Mine. Then again, how many times do you get to be thirty-five? Eleven? *(Pause.)* Okay, come on. Say it and get it over with. It's embarrassing. Quick. I can't stand it.

ALL *(except* BOBBIE). Happy Birthday, Bobbie.

BOBBIE. I stood it. Thank you for including me in your thoughts, your lives, your families. Yes, thank you for remembering. Thank you.

ALL (*except* BOBBIE). You don't look it.

BOBBIE. Well, I feel it.

ALL (*except* BOBBIE). It's the birthday girl!

BOBBIE. I see you've rehearsed. Very good. I am touched.

SUSAN (*speaking normally as do the others*). I love it when people are really surprised.

PETER. Susan loves it when people are really surprised.

SARAH (*handing* BOBBIE *a present*)....If you don't like it, you can take it back.

BOBBIE. Well, I haven't even seen it yet.

SARAH....I mean it, though, if you don't like it –

HARRY. Why don't you wait until she looks at the thing?

BOBBIE. I know I'll like it.

SARAH. Why don't you just take it back?

HARRY. For God's sake, she just said she likes it.

SARAH. Pretend not to notice Harry, sweetheart. I think I'll leave.

HARRY. I was being funny, Sarah. We could stay a little longer.

SUSAN. Hey, Bobbie, take mine and Peter's back too.

PAUL. Here's from Jamie and me. If I were you, I would take it back and get the money. It cost so much I almost passed out.

JAMIE. Paul, it did not, Bobbie.

PAUL. For a sweater?

JAMIE. You told her what it was!

PAUL (*to* BOBBIE). When I saw the price tag, I thought it was a Lamborghini.

JOANNE (*to* PAUL). Mister, mister. YOU! Yes, you! Tell her to take yours back and get the money. It's not the gift, it's the cost that counts.

PETER (*to* BOBBIE). Who *is* that?

JOANNE. That is I, sir. I am very rich and – (*Indicating* LARRY.) I am married to him, and I'd introduce him, but I forgot his name.

LARRY. Many happy returns of the day, kiddo.

JENNY. David is now going to deliver our greeting. Go on, darling.

DAVID. Bobbie. Happy birthday from us.

JENNY. ...and the kids!

DAVID *unrolls a 'Happy Birthday' banner.*

ALL (*except* BOBBIE). Happy birthday!

DAVID. And may this year bring you fame, fortune and your first husband.

ALL (*except* BOBBIE). Here, here.

BOBBIE. Listen, I'm fine without the three.

JOANNE. You bet your ass, baby. Tell it like it is.

BOBBIE. All right. Let's cut out the many happy returns and that is about enough about me. I am just indeed lucky enough to have all of you. I mean, when you've got friends like mine...

JAMIE *enters with a cake and begins to sing 'Happy Birthday'. The* COUPLES *join in. They finish the song and then they speak, call, applaud:*

ALL (*except* BOBBIE). Yeah! Hooray! (*Etc.*)

JAMIE. Blow out your candles and make a wish.

JENNY. Don't tell your wish, Bobbie, or it won't come true.

SUSAN. You have to close your eyes and blow them all out.

SARAH. Be sure you make it a good one.

BOBBIE *closes her eyes, wishes, blows, but the candles stay lit. As the following lines are spoken, each* COUPLE *begins to exit. By the time the singing starts,* BOBBIE *is alone. Music begins.*

JENNY. You still get your wish. She still gets her wish.

SUSAN. She does? It must be a new rule!

SARAH....Sure you do.

JOANNE. Don't believe a word of it.

JAMIE. Of course you do.

BOBBIE. Oh I know it. I will. Actually, I didn't wish for anything.

LARRY. She's kidding. You've got to be kidding.

DAVID. Anyway, don't tell it.

JOANNE. Tell it if it's dirty.

PAUL. They say you're not supposed to tell it.

JAMIE. Paul's right. Don't tell.

HARRY. Anyway, Bobbie, you're in your prime – thirty-five.

SARAH. Harry, hush! You don't tell a woman's age at our ages.

The COUPLES *re-enter, appearing individually on their first line. The following lines overlap.*

DAVID.
     Bobbie...

JENNY.
     Bobbie...

PAUL.
     Bobbie baby...

PETER.
     Bobbie honey...

SUSAN.
     Boo boo...

JOANNE.
Bobbie darling…

HARRY.
Bobbie, we've been trying to call you.

JAMIE.
Bobbie…

LARRY.
Bobbie…

PAUL.
Bobbie sugar…

JENNY.
Bobbie sweetie…

SARAH.
Angel, I've got something to tell you.

SUSAN.
Sweetheart…

JOANNE.
Kiddo…

HARRY.
Bobbie, love…

PETER.
Bobbie, honey…

JAMIE *and* PAUL.
Bobbie, we've been trying to reach you all day.

LARRY.
Bobbie…

SARAH.
Angel…

HARRY.
Bobbie…

JOANNE.
Darling…

DAVID.
> Bobbie baby…

HARRY.
> Bobbie…

SUSAN.
> Bobbie…

DAVID *and* JENNY.
> The kids were asking, Bobbie…

PETER.
> Honey…

JOANNE.
> Kiddo…

LARRY *and* JOANNE.
> Bobbie, there was something we wanted to say.

JAMIE.
> Sweetheart…

SARAH *and* HARRY.
> Bobbie…

SUSAN.
> Sugar…

PAUL.
> Bobbie baby…

PETER.
> What have you been up to, honey?

DAVID *and* JENNY.
> We left a message.

JAMIE *and* PAUL.
> Bobbie, Bobbie, how have you been?

HARRY.
> Lovey…

SARAH.
> Sweetie,

HARRY *and* SARAH.
How have you been?

PETER *and* SUSAN.
Bobbie, Bobbie, how have you been?

DAVID, JENNY, JOANNE *and* LARRY.
Stop by on your way home.

JAMIE *and* PAUL.
Seems like weeks since we talked to you –

HARRY *and* SARAH.
Bobbie, we've been thinking of you –

PETER *and* SUSAN.
Bobbie, we've been thinking of you –

DAVID, JENNY, JOANNE *and* LARRY.
Drop by any time!

JAMIE *and* PAUL.
Bobbie, there's a concert on Tuesday.

DAVID *and* JENNY.
Hank and Mary get into town tomorrow.

PETER *and* SUSAN.
How about some Scrabble on Sunday?

SARAH *and* HARRY.
Why don't we all go to the beach next weekend?

JOANNE *and* LARRY.
Come, we're having people in Saturday night.

JENNY.
Bobbie…

PETER.
Bobbie…

JAMIE.
Bobbie…

PAUL.
Bobbie…

SUSAN.
>Boo boo…

SARAH.
>Angel…

DAVID *and* JENNY.
>Whatcha doing Thursday?

PAUL.
>Bobbie baby…

SARAH *and* HARRY.
>Time we got together, is Wednesday all right?

JAMIE.
>Bobbie…

LARRY.
>Sweetheart…

SUSAN.
>Boo boo, call us…

JOANNE.
>Bobbie, darling…

JAMIE *and* PAUL.
>Eight o'clock on Monday.

PETER.
>Bobbie honey…

PETER *and* JOANNE.
>Bobbie baby…

ALL (*except* BOBBIE).
>Bobbie, come on over for dinner!
>We'll be so glad to see you!
>Bobbie, come on over for dinner!
>Just be the three of us,
>Only the three of us!
>We looooove you!

BOBBIE.
>Phone rings, door chimes, in comes company!
>No strings, good times, room hums, company!

Late nights, quick bites, party games,
Deep talks, long walks, telephone calls,
Thoughts shared, souls bared, private names,
All those photos up on the walls
'With love,'
With love filling the days,
With love seventy ways,
'To Bobbie, with love'
From all
Those
Good and crazy people, my friends,
Those
Good and crazy people, my married friends!
And that's what it's all about, isn't it?
That's what it's really about,
Really about!

THEO, PJ *and* ANDY *enter. The following lines overlap.*

ANDY.
    Bobbie…

THEO.
    Bobbie…

PJ.
    Bobbie baby…

PETER.
    Bobbie honey…

JOANNE.
    Darling…

SUSAN.
    Boo boo, sweetie…

SARAH *and* HARRY.
    Angel, will you do us a favour?

LARRY.
    Bobbie…

JAMIE.
    Bobbie…

JENNY.
    Bobbie baby…

PAUL.
    Bobbie, sweetheart…

BOBBIE.
    Tell me, Sarah.

PETER.
    Bobbie love, I'd like your opinion…

HARRY.
    Doll…

LARRY.
    Pumpkin…

PJ.
    Bobbie, girl…

THEO.
    Bobbie, honey…

BOBBIE.
    Try me, Peter…

LARRY *and* JAMIE.
    Bobbie, there's a problem, I need your advice…

ANDY *and* PAUL.
    Bobbie…

SARAH.
    Angel…

THEO *and* HARRY.
    Bobbie…

JOANNE.
    Darling…

PJ *and* PETER.
    Bobbie baby…

BOBBIE.
    Jamie, can I call you back tomorrow?

ANDY, PJ *and* THEO.
>Just half an hour…

DAVID *and* JENNY.
>Honey, if you'd visit the kids once or twice…

SARAH *and* PETER.
>Bobbie…

PAUL.
>Sweetheart…

JOANNE *and* HARRY.
>Bobbie…

SUSAN.
>Sugar…

JAMIE.
>Bobbie baby…

BOBBIE.
>Jenny, I could take them to the zoo on Friday.

ANDY, PJ *and* THEO.
>What's happened to you?

WIVES.
>Bobbie… Bobbie… where have you been?

HUSBANDS.
>Honey… kiddo… where have you been?

ANDY, PJ *and* THEO.
>Bobbie… Bobbie… where have you been?

BOBBIE.
>Susan, love, I'll make it after seven if I can.

HARRY, SARAH, PETER *and* SUSAN.
>Stop by on your way home…

WIVES.
>Bobbie, dear, I don't mean to pry…

HUSBANDS.
>Bobbie, we've been thinking of you!

ANDY, PJ *and* THEO.
> Bobbie, we've been thinking of you!

HARRY, SARAH, PETER *and* SUSAN.
> Drop by any time...

BOBBIE.
> Sorry, Paul, I made a date with Larry and Joanne.

WIVES.
> Bobbie dear, it's none of my business...

HUSBANDS.
> Listen, pal, I have to work Thursday evening...

WIVES.
> Darling, you've been looking peculiar...

HUSBANDS.
> Bobbie love, you know how I hate the opera...

WIVES.
> Funny thing, your name came up only last night.

BOBBIE.
> Harry... David... Theo, I... Andy... PJ... Listen, people...

ANDY, PJ *and* THEO.
> I shouldn't say this but...

WIVES.
> Bobbie, we've been worried, you sure you're all right?

HUSBANDS.
> Bobbie... Bobbie... Bobbie baby... Bobbie, sweetie...
> Bobbie, honey... Bobbie, Bobbie...

ANDY, PJ *and* THEO.
> Did I do something wrong?

ALL (*except* BOBBIE).
> Bobbie, come on over for dinner!
> We'll be so glad to see you!
> Bobbie, come on over for dinner!
> Just be the three of us,
> Only the three of us,
> We loooooove you!

ALL.

>Phone rings, door chimes, in comes company!
>No strings, good times, just chums, company!
>Late nights, quick bites, party games,
>Deep talks, long walks, telephone calls,
>Thoughts shared, souls bared, private names,
>All those photos up on the walls
>'With love,'
>With love filling the days,
>With love seventy ways,
>'To Bobbie, with love'
>From all
>These (Those)
>Good and crazy people, your (my) friends,
>These (Those) good and crazy people, your (my) married
>   friends!
>And that's what it's all about, isn't it?
>That's what it's really about, isn't it?
>That's what it's really about, really a–

HUSBANDS *and* WIVES.

>–bout...?

ANDY, PJ *and* THEO.

>Isn't it? Isn't it? Isn't it? Isn't it?

HUSBANDS *and* WIVES.

>Love!

ANDY, PJ *and* THEO.

>Isn't it? Isn't it? Isn't it? Isn't it?

BOBBIE.

>You I love and you I love and you and you I love
>And you I love and you I love and you and you
>I love, I love...

ALL.

>Company! Company! Company,
>Lots of company!
>Life is company!
>Love is company!
>Company!

A montage of city sounds is heard as the following lines are spoken quickly, overlapping each other, as the COMPANY *exits.*

SARAH. Harry, it's the door. I'll get it.

HARRY. I've got it.

SARAH. *I'll* get it. I always do.

JOANNE. What was that clock chime?

LARRY. Five o'clock.

JOANNE. Thank God, cocktail hour!

ANDY. Final departure call for American Airlines Flight 142. Will the passengers that have not boarded please do so.

PETER. What the hell is that noise?

SUSAN. They're either cleaning the building next door or tearing it down.

THEO. Taxi! Taxi! Oh, please, please!

PJ. Will you stop blowing that horn, you dodo!

JAMIE. Paul, what is that noise?

PAUL. I don't hear anything.

DAVID. Oh, Jenny, the phone.

JENNY. I'm getting it.

DAVID. Oh, the kids. It's gonna wake up the kids.

BOBBIE *suddenly finds herself alone for a moment.*

Scene Two

SARAH *and* HARRY*'s living room.* SARAH, HARRY *and*
BOBBIE *have finished a long dinner and are having coffee in
the living room.*

SARAH (*pouring coffee*). There's cinnamon in the coffee,
    Bobbie... the odd taste is cinnamon. Sugar and cream?

BOBBIE. Both.

HARRY. Do you want some brandy in it?

BOBBIE. You having some?

SARAH. We don't drink, but you have some, darling. Go
    ahead.

HARRY. Or do you want a real drink? We have anything you
    want.

BOBBIE. Well, Harry, if you don't mind, could I have some of
    the bourbon?

HARRY. Right.

SARAH. Sweetheart!

HARRY. Okay, darling.

BOBBIE (*as* HARRY *pours the bourbon*). Are you both on the
    wagon? Sarah? You're not on the wagon?

SARAH. Goodness, Bobbie, all the questions! Or do you just
    collect trivia like some old quiz-show contestant? We spend
    half of our lives with you and now you notice Harry's on the
    wagon?

HARRY. A year and a half.

SARAH. No, love. Just a year.

HARRY. It was a year in February. It's a year and a half now.

SARAH. I know for a fact next month it will be a year.

HARRY. And a half.

SARAH. One year. Count it, one! Harry got arrested for being drunk and quit out of some kind of humiliation.

HARRY. I quit to see if I could is actually what happened. C'mon, I must have told you about all that.

BOBBIE. Never. You never mentioned it or I never would have brought the bourbon. How were you arrested?

SARAH. Another question! Here, why don't you have one of these brownies you brought?

HARRY. I was in California on business and I really got soused one night and these guys drove me back to my hotel but instead of going in, I walked down to the corner to get something to eat to sober up.

SARAH. You said it was three blocks.

HARRY. No, just the corner.

SARAH. Three blocks.

HARRY. Anyway, this patrol car stopped me and said, 'You're drunk.' I said, 'Drunk? I'm clobbered.' He said, 'I'm taking you in.' 'Take me to my hotel, for God's sake,' I said, 'it's just on the corner.'

SARAH. Three blocks away.

HARRY. Anyway, they booked me for being drunk. Unbelievable Southern California is a Police state. In New York, or any place else, they would have put you in a cab and sent you home or something. And then, Bobbie, the very next time I was out there, I got arrested all over again – drunk driving. I only had wine –

SARAH. Only three bottles...

HARRY. And I *insisted* on taking a drunk test. I flunked it by one point.

SARAH. And that is when you quit, precious. He always thinks it was the first arrest, but it was the second. We never told you that? Curious, I thought Harry had told *everybody*.

HARRY. Anyway, I quit to see if I really had a drinking problem, and I don't.

SARAH. Just a problem drinking.

BOBBIE. Do you miss it?

SARAH. See how you talk in questions! Harry, do you miss it?

HARRY. No. No, I really don't.

SARAH. Yes. Yes, he really does. Hi, darling.

HARRY. Anyway, I stopped, haven't had a drink since.

SARAH. Whoops.

HARRY. What's whoops? I haven't had a drink since.

SARAH. At Sheila and George's wedding.

HARRY. A toast, for God's sake. Sorry, Bobbie, you must have noticed how staggering falling-down drunk I got on one swallow of Champagne.

SARAH. I never said you got drunk, but you did have the Champagne.

HARRY. A swallow. One swallow.

SARAH. And it was gone. An elephant swallow.

BOBBIE. I'd like to ask for another bourbon, but I'm terrified.

SARAH. Darling Bobbie, put a nipple on the bottle for all we care. Don't you want a brownie?

BOBBIE. God, no. I'll bust.

SARAH. Bust? You bust! You skinny thing. Just look at you. There's nothing to you. Bones. You're skin and bones. I bet when you get on a scale it goes the other way – minus.

BOBBIE. Well, thank you, Sarah. I think I was just insulted.

SARAH. Oh, Bobbie, I was praying that you'd eat just one so I could watch.

BOBBIE. Have you become a food voyeur?

SARAH. Mexican food. What I crave is Mexican food. With all the Tabasco sauce in the world.

HARRY. Don't eat that brownie!

SARAH. I'm not. I'm just smelling it. Oh, Bobbie, you eat one!

BOBBIE. Not with bourbon.

SARAH. And chocolate. I'd kill for chocolate. Or a baked potato with sour cream and chives. Doesn't that just make you writhe? Or hot sourdough bread and all the butter there is.

HARRY. Chili.

SARAH. Oh, chili, dear God, yes, chili!

HARRY. Manicotti.

SARAH. Manicotti. One teaspoon of manicotti.

HARRY. How about sweet and sour shrimp?

SARAH. How about sweet and sour anything?

> SARAH *pretends to pass out, and sticks a brownie in her mouth as she slides under the table. She eats it, thinking she is hidden from sight. As* BOBBIE *watches her,* HARRY *downs bourbon from the bottle. Then both* SARAH *and* HARRY *casually turn, their attention now back on* BOBBIE.

BOBBIE. I get the impression you two are on diets.

HARRY. Not me, Sarah.

SARAH. Look at these pants. You can put your fist in there. That's how much weight I've lost.

HARRY. She always does that. Look, I can put my fist in my pants too, you know. She thinks I buy that.

SARAH. Darling, I've lost eight pounds already.

BOBBIE. I am some gift-giver. Bourbon for Harry and brownies for Sarah!

HARRY. It's the magazines, Bobbie. Did you ever notice how many of the pages are dedicated to cakes and pies and roasts and potatoes? I bet Sarah subscribes to about forty magazines. It's a sickness. We're up to our ass in magazines.

SARAH. I read them all.

HARRY. Don't.

SARAH. Do.

HARRY. Look at this, Bobbie. Wrestling. She even subscribes to a magazine on wrestling.

SARAH. Jiu-jitsu, not wrestling. It's jiu-jitsu. Strangely enough, darling, I'm terribly good at it.

BOBBIE. How long have you been studying it?

SARAH. Who asked that question? Oh, Bobbie! Seven months.

HARRY. Show us some jiu-jitsu.

SARAH. No. Bobbie, would you like some more coffee? You, Harry?

HARRY. No. I want some jiu-jitsu.

SARAH. No.

BOBBIE. Do one thing.

SARAH. No.

BOBBIE. Come on, Sarah, I really would give anything to see you do just one. I bet you are excellent. Hey, I'll be your partner.

SARAH. No. Oh, Harry, this is embarrassing.

HARRY. Aw, come on.

SARAH. My God – all right.

HARRY. Hooray!

SARAH. One throw!

HARRY. Hooray!

SARAH. Harry, do you want to stand there?

HARRY. Where?

SARAH. There.

HARRY. All right. I'm standing here. Now what?

SARAH *goes into her jiu-jitsu preparation ritual.*

SARAH. Okay. Now just come at me.

HARRY. Okay.

> HARRY *goes at her and she lets out a piercing samurai sound, flipping him to the floor.*

BOBBIE. Fantastic. That's hysterical.

HARRY. Actually, I could have prevented that.

SARAH. How?

HARRY. By blocking it.

SARAH. No, that can't be blocked.

HARRY. It certainly can. I just didn't do it.

SARAH. Anyway, Bobbie, that can't be blocked.

HARRY. Let's do it again.

SARAH. All right, darling.

HARRY. I'll come at you again.

SARAH. Okay.

> *He goes at her. She attempts the same thing and he blocks it.*

> Oh, I see. Put me down. Okay, do it again.

> *He does it again and she overcomes his block, throwing him again. She then screams and jumps on top of him, holding him down.* JOANNE *appears and looks at them for a moment.*

JOANNE.
> It's the little things you do together,
> Do together,
> Do together,
> That make perfect relationships.
> The hobbies you pursue together,
> Savings you accrue together,
> Looks you misconstrue together
> That make marriage a joy.
> Mm-hm...

BOBBIE. That's very good.

HARRY. Once more. Do it once more.

BOBBIE. Harry, could I have another bourbon?

> HARRY *lunges at* SARAH. *They block each other and are caught in a power struggle.*

SARAH. Give up?

HARRY. Do you?

SARAH. I've got you.

HARRY. I've got *you.*

SARAH. All right. You break first.

HARRY. Uh-uh. You break first.

SARAH. We can just stay here.

HARRY. All right with me. Fine with me.

BOBBIE. You're both very good.

BOTH. Thank you.

HARRY. I could get out of this, you know.

SARAH. Try it.

> HARRY *kicks a foot behind* SARAH's *feet, knocking her to the floor. Then he gets on top of her, pinning her down.*

HARRY. Okay, I tried it.

> SARAH *throws* HARRY *to the floor. She gets up, grabs his arm, and, with her foot in his armpits, pins him down.*

SARAH. Uncle?

HARRY. Uncle, your ass!

JOANNE.
> It's the little things you share together,
> Swear together,
> Bear together,
> That make perfect relationships.

The concerts you enjoy together,
Neighbours you annoy together,
Children you destroy together,
That keep marriage intact.

It's not so hard to be married
When two manoeuvre as one.
It's not so hard to be married,
And, Omigod, is it fun.

It's sharing little winks together,
Drinks together,
Kinks together,
That make marriage a joy.

It's bargains that you shop together,
Cigarettes you stop together,
People that you drop together
That make perfect relationships.

Uh-huh...
Mm-hm...

SARAH *and* HARRY *break and prepare for a third fall.*

BOBBIE. Could I have another bourbon?

BOBBIE *is hit from the front and rear by* HARRY *and* SARAH. HARRY *and* SARAH *pin* BOBBIE *on the sofa. The* COUPLES *enter and sing with* JOANNE.

ALL.
It's not wedded bliss and what happens in bed that
Allows you to get through the worst.
It's 'I do' and 'You don't' and 'Nobody said that'
And 'Who brought the subject up first?'
It's the little things...
The little things, the little things, the little things...

SUSAN *and* PETER.
The little ways you try together,

JAMIE *and* PAUL.
Cry together,

JENNY *and* DAVID.
Lie together

ALL.
That make perfect relationships,

SUSAN, PETER, JAMIE *and* PAUL.
Becoming a cliché together,

JENNY *and* DAVID.
Growing old and grey together,

JOANNE.
Withering away together

ALL.
That makes marriage a joy.

MEN *and* JOANNE.
It's not so hard to be married,

WOMEN (*except* JOANNE).
It's much the simplest of crimes.

ALL.
It's not so hard to be married,

JOANNE.
I've done it three or four times.

JENNY *and* DAVID.
It's people that you hate together,

JAMIE *and* PAUL.
Bait together,

SUSAN *and* PETER.
Date together,

ALL.
That make marriage a joy.

DAVID.
It's things like using force together,

LARRY.
Shouting till you're hoarse together,

JOANNE.
> Getting a divorce together,

ALL.
> That make perfect relationships.
> Uh-huh...
> Kiss, kiss...

JOANNE.
> Mm-hm.

JOANNE and the COUPLES *exit.* BOBBIE, SARAH *and* HARRY *break.*

BOBBIE. Why... wow... how 'bout that? Huh?

HARRY. I had you there...

SARAH. I had *you* there...

They start for each other again, but BOBBIE *steps between them.*

BOBBIE. I'd say it was a draw. Wow. Look at the time. I've got to get going.

SARAH *and* HARRY. Awwww!

BOBBIE. Wow. Listen, I had a great time.

SARAH. So did we.

HARRY. Terrific to see you. Sure you wouldn't care for a nightcap?

BOBBIE. Right! I mean, no! I mean, will I see you guys soon?

SARAH. Don't answer that, Harry. She gets no more questions.

BOBBIE *turns to exit, stops.*

BOBBIE (*to herself*). Wow.

Underscoring: 'Bobbie Baby' music.

BOBBIE *begins to leave.* SARAH *picks up the plate of brownies. Before making a full exit,* BOBBIE *stops and observes the following moment between* SARAH *and* HARRY.

HARRY. I'll turn out the lights.

SARAH. I will! I always do.

HARRY. No, you don't.

As SARAH *begins to exit, she turns to catch* HARRY *reaching for the bottle of bourbon.*

SARAH. Oh, Harry, you sly old thing.

She exits, stuffing a brownie into her mouth. HARRY *pours himself a large bourbon.*

BOBBIE. Harry! You ever sorry you got married?

HARRY.
>You're always sorry,
>You're always grateful,
>You're always wondering what might have been.
>Then she walks in.
>
>And still you're sorry,
>And still you're grateful,
>And still you wonder and still you doubt,
>And she goes out.
>
>Everything's different,
>Nothing's changed,
>Only maybe slightly
>Rearranged.
>
>You're sorry-grateful,
>Regretful-happy,
>Why look for answers where none occur?
>You always are what you always were,
>Which has nothing to do with,
>All to do with her.

SARAH (*offstage*). Harry, darling, come to bed.

HARRY. Coming, darling.

DAVID appears and sings.

DAVID.
>You're always sorry,
>You're always grateful,

You hold her thinking, 'I'm not alone.'
You're still alone.

You don't live for her,
You do live with her,
You're scared she's starting to drift away
And scared she'll stay.

LARRY *enters*.

LARRY.
Good things get better,
Bad get worse.
Wait – I think I meant that in reverse.

HARRY, LARRY *and* DAVID.
You're sorry-grateful,
Regretful-happy,
Why look for answers where none occur?
You'll always be what you always were,
Which has nothing to do with, all to do with her.

DAVID *exits*.

HARRY *and* LARRY.
You'll always be what you always were,
Which has nothing to do with, all to do with her.

LARRY *exits*.

HARRY.
Nothing to do with,
All to do with her.

Scene Three

PETER *and* SUSAN*'s apartment.* BOBBIE *stands alone on the terrace.*

SUSAN. Bobbie?

BOBBIE. Out here.

PETER. For Chrissake, what are you doing out here?

BOBBIE. Oh, it is so nice to have a terrace in this city.

SUSAN. Yes! Though we just use it to store old sleds and stuff. Look. Hundreds of thousands of terraces in New York and never have I seen a single person out on even one of them.

BOBBIE. You don't ever just sit out here?

PETER. I hate it. And the kids are impossible out here.

SUSAN. . . . And everyone can hear everything you say. (*Leans over, calls up.*) Are you listening? (*To* PETER *and* BOBBIE.) And it's dirty all the time. Look at all the bird-doo.

PETER. And noisy?!! You can't even hear yourself think. And what can you see? It's not like you see something. All you can see is the building across the street.

SUSAN (*leaning over*). Well, if you lean way out and look over there you can see the East River.

PETER (*pulling* SUSAN *back*). Except that you really can't. Susan almost met her maker one night trying to see that river. She did. It's a miracle she's alive today.

BOBBIE. You saved her?

PETER. Me? No. Well, I suppose, in a way.

SUSAN. He fainted so I got down.

PETER. Blood and heights – I always faint. And that night she was out there on her knees, way out there – I can't even talk about it. Susan's not afraid of anything at all. One day she fell off the ladder when she was putting up our Christmas lights and she split her head right open. Well. I fainted. I came to, I examined her head and I fainted again.

SUSAN. Four times he fainted that night.

PETER (*laughing*). Four!

BOBBIE (*laughing*). Well, see now, to me that is really charming. You are one lucky girl, Susan. You two are – she said with envy – just beautiful together. Really. And Susan – if you ever decide to leave him – I want to be the first to know.

PETER. Well...

SUSAN. You're the first to know.

PETER. We're getting divorced.

SUSAN. We haven't told anyone yet.

BOBBIE (*stunned*). Oh.

Underscoring: 'Bobbie Baby' music.

I'm – uh, so surprised.

SUSAN *and* PETER *stand smiling, just looking at* BOBBIE.

Maybe you'll work it out.

Pause.

Don't think so, huh? (*To* PETER.) Well, I'm sure nobody can imagine how you feel. (*To* SUSAN.) Or *you* feel. (*Turning; to herself, as she begins to exit.*) Or *I* feel.

(*Once alone.*) Wow.

Scene Four

On the steps outside JENNY *and* DAVID*'s apartment.* JENNY, BOBBIE *and* DAVID *are smoking a joint.*

DAVID. Feel? I just don't feel anything. Here, Bobbie, I don't care for any more. It's too small. That's too small. It probably just doesn't work on me. Do you feel anything, Jenny? Do you, honey? Because I don't.

BOBBIE. You will.

DAVID. *When!* I mean, we've had *two* for Christ's sake. I think maybe it depends on a person's constitution. Don't you, Jen? But hey, it's always good to try everything once.

BOBBIE. Just wait!

DAVID. I'm not planning to go anywhere. Maybe I'm just too square, but I honestly don't feel anything. Do you, Jen? Honestly, not a thing. I mean, I *wish* I did. I just don't. Maybe they gave you *real* grass, right off the front lawn. I knew I wouldn't feel anything. I don't have that kind of constitution. Why am I talking so much?

BOBBIE. You're stoned.

DAVID. I am not.

JENNY. I am.

DAVID. Are you, Jen? You are not. I'm so dry!

BOBBIE. You're stoned.

DAVID. Is that supposed to be part of it?

BOBBIE. You'll probably get hungry too.

DAVID. Yes? Should I feel *that*, too?

BOBBIE. You don't have to feel anything.

DAVID. Are you hungry, Jen?

JENNY. No. I'd like some water, though.

DAVID. Me, too. Do you want some, Bobbie?

BOBBIE. No, thank you.

DAVID. What?

BOBBIE. I already have some, David, thank you.

DAVID. Some what, Bobbie?

JENNY. You asked her, honey. Water!

DAVID. Oh, water... I could not remember what we were talking about.

BOBBIE. See, you forget when you're high!

DAVID. Ohhhh. God, do you. Wow. Are you high, Jen?

JENNY. I'm potted.

DAVID. Potted. That is beautiful. Jesus!

BOBBIE. Trust me, you're high.

DAVID. Jesus!

JENNY. That's twice you said 'Jesus'.

DAVID. You're kidding.

JENNY. No. You said it two times. He never swears, have you ever noticed?

DAVID. It's my Baptist upbringing.

JENNY. Say 'bitch.'

DAVID (*after a hesitation*). Bitch.

They all laugh.

JENNY. Say 'Kiss my ass.'

DAVID. Kiss my ass.

They roar at this.

Kiss my ass, you bitch.

They scream with laughter.

Oh, Jesus. That's three!

They laugh.

Shhh. Shhh. You'll wake the neighbours. Let's laugh to ourselves.

JENNY. Oh David, for God's sake.

DAVID. No, seriously! We'll get evicted!

BOBBIE. David, you're just wonderful. You're the guy I should have married.

DAVID. Listen, I know a great guy in this building you'd just love.

BOBBIE. What?

DAVID. When are you going to get married?

JENNY. What?

DAVID. I mean it. To me a person's not complete until they're married.

JENNY. She's complete enough. (*To* BOBBIE.) You're better off the way you are.

BOBBIE. So I hear.

DAVID. Oh, Jen. Do you mean that?

JENNY. No. (*Pause*.) Well, frankly, sometimes I'd like to be single.

DAVID. Oh. That's not even funny.

JENNY. It has nothing to do with you.

DAVID. I'm your husband!

JENNY. And that's the way I want it. But didn't you ever wish you could be single again? I mean for an hour even?

DAVID. No. (*Pause*.) Could you make it two hours?

He and BOBBIE *laugh*.

Now, Bobbie, you get yourself married. See the ideas you're giving Jen.

BOBBIE. Oh, I will. It's not like I'm avoiding marriage. It's avoiding me, if anything. I'm ready.

DAVID. Actually you're not. But listen, not everybody should be married, I guess.

JENNY. I know what you're saying, David. If you're married, your life has a – what? What am I trying to say? A point to it – a bottom. I have everything – except freedom. Which is everything – huh? No. This is everything. I got my husband, my kids, a home, maybe you got to give up to get.

BOBBIE. Listen, I agree. I've thought a lot about being married. But you know what bothers me is, if you marry, then you've got another person there all the time. And, you can't get out of it whenever you just might want to get out of it. You are caught! And even if you do get out of it, what do you have to show for it? Not to mention the fact that – then – you've always been *married*. I mean, you can never *not* have been *married* again.

DAVID. I don't think you're really ready. Do you think, maybe subconsciously – you might be resisting it?

BOBBIE. No. Absolutely not! I have no block, no resistance. I am ready to be married.

DAVID. Then why aren't you?

Pause.

BOBBIE. I've always had things to accomplish. That's the main reason. First I had to finish school. Then I wanted to get started, to get some kind of a career. And, uh – just things I wanted to do before I could even begin to think in terms of marriage. Frankly I wanted to have some fun before I settled down.

JENNY. Right. Which is what you've been doing.

DAVID. Bobbie, honey, none of us are getting any younger.

BOBBIE. Right. (*Pause.*) Then why am I not with someone, huh? Wait though. You just wait. You are going to see major changes in my life. (*Starts swiping left continuously on her mobile phone.*) I mean I meet men all the time. All over the place. I mean living in New York you can meet a man a minute. And I've met some really special guys recently. Like right now, I'm seeing this flight attendant. Cute, original...

She shows them a picture. ANDY *appears as we hear underscoring of 'Bobbie Baby' music.*

...odd. And Theo, you guys never met Theo, did you? Well, he's extraordinary...

Another picture. THEO *appears.*

...I mean extraordinary! And then there's PJ.

Another picture. PJ *appears.*

God, now that boy's fun! (*Pause.*) Anyway, I'm certainly not resisting settling down! My life is totally prepared for a gigantic change right now. I am genuinely ready to be married.

DAVID. Right. Then why aren't you?

BOBBIE. Right!

PJ. Right!

ANDY. Right!

THEO. Right!

THEO, PJ *and* ANDY.
    Bah-dah da-dah...
    Bah-dah da-dah...
    Bah-dah da-daht daht dah...

    You could drive a person crazy,
    You could drive a person mad.
    Bah-dah dah!
    First you make a person feel all hazy
    So a person could be had.
    Bah-dah dah!
    Then you leave a person dangling sadly
    Outside your door,
    Which it only makes a person gladly
    Want you even more.

    I could understand a person
    If she said to go away.
    Bah-dah dah!

I could understand a person
If she happened to be gay.

ANDY.
You think?

THEO.
Do I know?

PJ.
Nah.

THEO, PJ *and* ANDY.
But worse'n that,
A person that
Titillates a person and then leaves him flat
Is crazy,
She's a troubled person,
She's a truly crazy person
Herself!

Ad lib insults, such as:

PJ. Dirty flirt.

THEO. You 'feminist'.

ANDY. Just don't understand.

THEO. That time of the month?

PJ. Ginger monster.

THEO (*with* PJ *and* ANDY*'s 'doo-doo' backing vocals underneath*).
When a person's personality is personable,
She shouldn't oughta sit on her butt.
It's harder than a matador coercin' a bull
To try to get you outta your rut.

THEO, PJ *and* ANDY.
So single and attentive and attractive a chick
Is everything a person could wish,
But turning off a person is the act of a chick
Who likes to pull the hooks out of fish.

>Knock, knock, is anybody there?
>Knock, knock, it really isn't –

ANDY.
>– fair…

PJ.
>Not fair…

THEO.
>Not fair…

THEO, PJ *and* ANDY.
>Not fair!

>Knock, knock, I'm working all my charms.
>Knock, knock, a zombie's in my arms.
>All that sweet affection,
>What is wrong?
>Where's the loose connection?
>How long, oh Lord, how long?
>Bobbie baby, Bobbie bubi, Bobbie,

>You could drive a person frantic,
>You could blow a person's cool.
>Like you get a person all romantic,
>While you make him feel a fool.
>Bah-dah!

>When a person says you just don't get her,
>That's when you're good.
>You impersonate a person better
>Than a zombie should.

>I could understand a person
>If she wasn't good in bed.

THEO. She's good.

PJ *and* ANDY. No shit.

THEO, PJ *and* ANDY.
>I could understand a person
>If she actually was dead.
>Bah-dah dah-dah!

Exclusive you,
Elusive you,
Will any person ever get the juice of you?
You're crazy,
You're a troubled person,
You're a moving, deeply maladjusted,
Never to be trusted
Crazy person
Yourself.

Bobbie is my hobby and I'm giving it up.

They exit.

DAVID. Oh Bobbie, you don't have to defend yourself. Not at all – ever. It's no business of ours anyway. Is it, Jen? Why are we going on and on about it? I'm starving. I'll get us something to eat. (*Gets up.*) Do one of you bitches want to help? Then kiss my ass. (*Laughs with* BOBBIE.) I haven't laughed like that in ages.

DAVID *and* BOBBIE *fall about laughing again.*

BOBBIE (*to* DAVID). You're funny when you're high. You really loosen up!

JENNY. Oh boy.

BOBBIE. Should I roll another one?

DAVID. Maybe one.

JENNY. No.

BOBBIE. I can roll another in a second.

JENNY. No.

DAVID. No more?

JENNY. I don't think so.

Pause.

DAVID. I don't think so either.

BOBBIE. It'll just take a second to make another one.

JENNY. Listen, you two have one.

DAVID. I don't want one.

JENNY. Have one if you want one.

DAVID. But I don't.

> I'll get some food. (*Embraces* JENNY.) Isn't she a marvellous woman?

JENNY. I married a square. A registered square.

> DAVID *turns to exit, then turns back.*

DAVID. Bobbie, we're just too old! We were all – trying to be kids again tonight. Come on, we've been there already. Who wants to go back? It was hard enough getting this far. Anyway what do I know.

JENNY. Hey, husband. I'm starving.

DAVID. I love you… so much.

JENNY. Food!

DAVID. And, Bobbie, put that stuff away. Take it home. Come on.

> BOBBIE *puts it in her pocket or purse.*

> Thanks. I don't know, maybe you're right. Whoever knows?

> *He shrugs and exits.*

BOBBIE. What was all that?

JENNY. He doesn't go for it. I knew he wouldn't go for it.

BOBBIE. He was stoned.

JENNY. Not really. He doesn't get things like that. I mean, he'll go along with it, but that's all.

BOBBIE. He didn't like it?

JENNY. I know him. He was doing it for me.

BOBBIE. You want me to get *you* some?

JENNY. David would have a fit.

BOBBIE. He loved it.

JENNY. For me. He loved it for me. He didn't really love it. I know him. He's what he said... square... he doesn't want to be a kid anymore...

BOBBIE. Yeah. You could have fooled me!

Underscoring: 'Bobbie Baby' music.

JENNY. I'll see if I can give him a hand. What do you say?

She looks at BOBBIE *for a moment, then exits.*

BOBBIE. Wow. Oh, wow.

She starts to exit but is stopped by the COUPLES *who begin to appear. Their voices overlap.*

JENNY.
     Bobbie...

PETER.
     Bobbie...

JAMIE.
     Bobbie honey...

PAUL.
     Bobbie sweetie...

ALL (*except* BOBBIE).
     Bobbie...

SUSAN.
     Bobbie, darling...

HARRY, SARAH, DAVID, JENNY, PETER, SUSAN, PAUL *and* JOANNE.
     Bobbie, we've been trying to reach you...

LARRY.
     Bobbie...

JAMIE.
     Bobbie baby...

PAUL.
     Bobbie bubi...

SARAH.
> Angel, I've got something to tell you…

HARRY.
> Sweetie…

LARRY.
> Kiddo…

JOANNE.
> Bobbie love…

SUSAN.
> Bobbie honey…

JAMIE *and* PAUL.
> Bobbie, it's important or I wouldn't call…

JENNY.
> Bobbie…

PETER.
> Bobbie…

HARRY.
> Bobbie baby…

LARRY.
> Bobbie…

JOANNE.
> Honey…

HARRY, SARAH, DAVID, JENNY, PETER *and* SUSAN.
> Whatcha doing Thursday?

JOANNE *and* LARRY.
> Bobbie baby…

SARAH *and* HARRY.
> Bobbie, look, I know how you hate it and all…

JENNY.
> Darling…

DAVID.
> Sweetie…

JENNY *and* DAVID.
> Bobbie baby…

JENNY, DAVID, PAUL, LARRY *and* JOANNE.
> Not that you don't know a lot of lovely guys, but…

SARAH, HARRY, JAMIE, PETER *and* SUSAN.
> But this is something special!

ALL (*except* BOBBIE).
> Bobbie, come on over for dinner,
> There's someone we want you to meet.
> Bobbie come on over for dinner!

HUSBANDS.
> This guy from the office…

WIVES.
> My best friend from high school…

WIVES *and* HUSBANDS.
> It'll just be the four of us…
> You'll looooove him!

The HUSBANDS *leave. The* WIVES *and* JAMIE *corner*
BOBBIE.

JOANNE.
> Have I got a guy for you? Wait till you meet him!
> Have I got a guy for you, doll?
> Ooh, doll!
> Smart – but with a weakness for Sazerac slings.
> You give him even the fruit and he swings.
> The kind of stuff you can't send through the mails –
> Call me tomorrow, I want the details!

JENNY.
> Have I got the man for you? Wait till you meet him!
> Have I got the man for you, kid?
> Hoo, kid!
> Smooth – he's into all those exotic mystiques:
> The Kama Sutra and Chinese techniques –
> They say he knows more than seventy-five…
> Call me tomorrow if you're still alive!

WIVES *and* JAMIE.

>Have I got a guy for you? Wait till you meet him!
>Have I got a guy for you, girl?
>Hoo, girl!
>God, to be in your shoes what I wouldn't give.
>I mean the freedom to go out and live!
>And as for settling down and all that –
>Marriage may be where it's been,
>But it's not where it's at.
>
>What do you like, you like coming home to a kiss?
>Somebody with a smile at the door?
>What do you like, you like indescribable bliss?
>Then what do you want to get married for?
>
>What do you like, you like laughter filling your days,
>Somebody on your side ever more?
>What do you like, you like constant showers of praise?
>Then what do you want to get married for?
>What do you want to get married for?
>What do you want to get married for?
>What do you want to get married for?

The WIVES *and* JAMIE *exit, leaving* BOBBIE *alone onstage.*

BOBBIE.

>Someone is waiting,
>Sweet as David,
>Funny and charming as Peter.
>Larry…
>Someone is waiting,
>Cute as Jamie,
>Sassy as Harry
>And tender as Paul.
>
>Would I know him, even if I met him?
>Have I missed him? Did I let him go?
>A Peter sort of Larry,
>A David kind of Paul,
>Wait for me! I'm ready now!
>If you exist at all…

Someone will hold me,
Strong as David,
Silly but solid, like Peter –
Larry...
Someone will wake me,
Warm as David,
Loyal as Harry,
And loving as Paul.

Did I know him? Have I waited too long?
Maybe so, but maybe so has he,
My loyal Harry,
Loving Paul,
Cute Jamie,
Happy Peter,
Handsome Larry,
Wait for me.
I'll hurry,
Wait for me.
Hurry.
Wait for me.
Hurry.
Wait for me...

Scene Five

Lights come up on PJ.

PJ.

Another hundred people just got off of the train and came
  up through the ground
While another hundred people just got off of the bus and
  are looking around
At another hundred people who got off of the plane and
  are looking at us
Who got off of the train
And the plane and the bus
Maybe yesterday.

It's a city of strangers –
Some come to work, some to play –
A city of strangers –
Some come to stare, some to stay,
And every day
The ones who stay

Can find each other in the crowded streets and the
  guarded parks,
By the rusty fountains and the dusty trees with the
  battered barks,
And they walk together past the postered walls with the
  crude remarks.
And they meet at parties through the friends of friends
Who they never know.
Will you pick me up or do I meet you there or shall we let
  it go?
Did you get my message, 'cause I looked in vain?
Can we see each other Tuesday if it doesn't rain?
Look, I'll text you in the morning or I'll call you and
  explain…

And another hundred people just got off the train.

ANDY, *in a flight attendant's uniform, appears with*
BOBBIE. PJ *observes the following scene.*

ANDY. I didn't come right to New York. I went to
Northwestern University for two years but it was a pitiful
mistake. I was on probation the whole two years. I was
getting ready to go back to Shaker Heights when I decided
where I really wanted to live more than any other place was
– Radio City. I thought it was a wonderful little city near
New York. So I came here. I'm pretty dumb.

BOBBIE. You're not dumb, Andy.

ANDY. To me I am. Even the reason I stayed in New York was
because I just cannot get interested in myself – I'm so
boring. But in New York, see, I walk around and get
interested in other things and other people, and that way I get
involved. Or I sleep a lot.

BOBBIE. I find you very interesting.

ANDY. Well, I'm just not. I used to think I was so odd. But my
roommate is the same way. She's also pretty dumb.

BOBBIE. Oh, you never mentioned her. Is she – are you
involved?

ANDY. Oh, no. We just share this apartment on West End
Avenue. We have our own rooms and everything. I'd show it
to you but we've never had company. We're both very
private – and quiet and tired – she's the sweetest thing
actually. I think she likes the arrangement. I don't know
though – we never discuss it. She was born in New York – so
nothing really interests her. (*Pause*.) I don't have anything
more to say.

BOBBIE. What would you do if either of you ever got married?

ANDY. . . . Get a bigger place, I guess. (*Exits*.)

PJ.

> And they find each other in the crowded streets and the
> > guarded parks,
> By the rusty fountains and the dusty trees with the
> > battered barks,
> And they walk together past the postered walls with the
> > crude remarks.
> And they meet at parties through the friends of friends

Who they never know.
Will you pick me up or do I meet you there or shall we let
    it go?
Did you get my message, 'cause I looked in vain?
Can we see each other Tuesday if it doesn't rain?
Look, I'll text you in the morning or I'll call you and
    explain…

And another hundred people just got off of the train.

BOBBIE *is now seen with* THEO.

BOBBIE. This is really exciting, Theo. Fascinating.

THEO. Bobbie, you're awful.

BOBBIE. You come here a lot, huh? Swell. And maybe next
week we can go watch a haircut.

THEO. Oh, you just can't bear that with a big party going on
I talked you into coming here with me.

BOBBIE. What party are you – oh, *that* party. I'd completely
forgotten about that party. But hey, maybe we can still make it.

THEO. …Bobbie, try to enjoy this. We're in a park. A tiny
pocket of a park, right here in the middle of the busy, noisy
East Fifties. It's wondrously simple with that waterfall on the
wall that always makes me ache to be back up at the Cape.

BOBBIE. You really are a piece of work.

THEO. …What I am is like this park. Out of place.

BOBBIE. You are like this park. Very calming. Very.

THEO. …I used to dream I'd come to New York, have two
terrific affairs and then get married. I always knew I was
meant to be a husband.

BOBBIE. Then how come *we* never got married? Why did you
never ask me?

THEO. You wanted to marry me?

BOBBIE. I did. I honestly did… in the beginning. But I…
I don't know. I never thought that you would ask.

THEO. Oh, I would. I've never understood why you never asked me.

BOBBIE. So you wanted to marry me? And I wanted to marry you. Well then, how the hell did we ever end up such good friends?

THEO. Bobbie, I've never let you know what an incredible, incredible woman I think you are and how much you've meant. Bobbie, I...

Pause.

I brought you here because I wanted to tell you alone. I'm moving back up to Cape Cod. I'm getting married.

BOBBIE. Married?

THEO. Some people still get married, you know.

BOBBIE. Did you just suddenly fall in love?

Pause.

THEO. I'll be a good husband. I want real things now. A wife, a family. I don't want to keep running around this city like I'm having a life.

BOBBIE. Your problem is you want too little. That's the hardest thing in the world to get. (*Pause.*) Thank you for your park.

THEO. You're welcome. But, see, it and I, we just don't fit. I think there's a time to come to New York and a time to leave. Enjoy your party. (*Exits.*)

PJ.

    Another hundred people just got off of the train
    And came up through the ground
    While another hundred people just got off of the bus
    And are looking around
    At another hundred people who got off of the plane
    And are looking at us
    Who got off of the train
    And the plane and the bus
    Maybe yesterday.

It's a city of strangers –
Some come to work, some to play.
A city of strangers –
Some come to stare, some to stay,
And every day
Some go away...

Or they find each other in the crowded streets and the
    guarded parks,
By the rusty fountains and the dusty trees with the
    battered barks,
And they walk together past the postered walls with the
    crude remarks.
And they meet at parties through the friends of friends
Who they never know.
Will you pick me up or do I meet you there or shall we let
    it go?
Did you get my message, 'cause I looked in vain?
Can we see each other Tuesday if it doesn't rain?
Look, I'll text you in the morning or I'll call you and
    explain...

And another hundred people just got off of the train.

And another hundred people just got off of the train.
And another hundred people just got off of the train.
And another hundred people just got off of the train.
Another hundred people just got off of the train.

(*Sitting next to* BOBBIE.) You wanna know why I came to
New York? I came because New York is the centre of the
world and that's where I want to be. You know what the
pulse of this city is?

BOBBIE. A busy signal?

PJ. The pulse of this city, baby, is *me*. This city is for the me's
of the world. People that want to be right in the heart of it.
I am like the soul of New York.

BOBBIE. How about that?

PJ. See, smart remarks do not a person make. How many Puerto
Ricans do you know?

BOBBIE. Let's see...

PJ (*interrupting*). How many blacks?

BOBBIE. Well –

PJ. Man, talk about pathetic. Jews, Hispanics, the gays, Arabs, street people, all my closest, my best friends. Listen, I pass people on the street, yeah and I know them. Every son of a bitch is my friend. I go uptown, like to the dentist or something, and I swear, suddenly I want to cry because I think, 'Oh my God, I'm *uptown*.' But Fourteenth Street. Well, I don't know why anybody talks about anyplace *else*, because *that* is the centre of the universe.

BOBBIE. Fourteenth Street?

PJ. That's humanity, Fourteenth Street. That's everything.

BOBBIE. Well, God bless Fourteenth Street.

PJ. This city – I kiss the ground of it. Someday you know what I want to do? I want to get all dressed up in black – black sneaks, black skinnies, black fur coat, black hat, everything black – and go sit in some bar at the end of the counter, and just stare into my glass. That is my idea of honest-to-God sophistication. I mean, *that's* New York. (*Pause.*) You always make me feel like I got the next line. What is it with you?

BOBBIE. I just never met anybody like you.

PJ. Me neither. You know what this city is? Where a person can feel it? It's in a person's ass. If you're really part of this city, relaxed, cool and in the whole flow of it, your ass is like this. (*Makes a large round circle with his forefinger and thumb.*) If you're just living here, runnin' around uptight, not really part of this city, your ass is like this. (*Tightens the circle to nothing, making a fist.*)

BOBBIE. I... hesitate to ask...

PJ *holds the tight fist up high.*

That's a fascinating theory. And at this moment, extraordinarily accurate.

BOBBIE *exits.*

Scene Six

A female PRIEST *in a white choir robe appears.*

PRIEST.
> Bless this day, pinnacle of joy,
> Boy unites with boy.
> The heart leaps up to behold
> This golden day.

The PRIEST *disappears.*

Lights come up on JAMIE*'s kitchen.* JAMIE *is shining a pair of black shoes.* PAUL *appears.*

PAUL. Jamie, I can't find my shoes any –

> (*Suddenly expansively romantic.*)
> Today is for Jamie.
> Jamie, I give you the rest of my days,
> To cherish and to keep you,
> To honour you forever.
> Today is for Jamie,
> My lover, my partner, my life.

(*Spoken.*) Hey, buddy, we're really getting married!

PAUL *exits;* JAMIE *shakes his head 'yes' and it becomes 'no'.*

JAMIE (*to the audience*).
> Pardon me, is everybody there?
> Because if everybody's there
> I want to thank you all for coming to the wedding.
> I'd appreciate your going even more,
> I mean you must have lots of better things to do,
> And not a word of it to Paul. Remember Paul?
> You know, the man I'm gonna marry,
> But I'm not because I wouldn't ruin
> Anyone as wonderful as he is –
>
> But I thank you all
> For the gifts and the flowers.
> Thank you all,
> Now it's back to the showers.

Don't tell Paul,
But, I'm not getting married today.

The PRIEST *reappears.*

PRIEST.
Bless this day, opposite of joy,
Boy gets yoked to boy.
The heart sinks down and feels dead,
This dreadful day.

The PRIEST *disappears.*

BOBBIE *appears, dressed as the Maid of Honour.*

BOBBIE. Jamie, Paul can't find his good cufflinks.

JAMIE. On the dresser.

BOBBIE *exits.*

Right next to my suicide note.

(*To the audience, sings.*)
Listen everybody,
Look, I don't know what you're waiting for.
A wedding, what's a wedding?
It's a prehistoric ritual
Where everybody promises fidelity forever,
Which is maybe the most horrifying word I've ever heard,
And which is followed by a honeymoon
Where suddenly he'll realise
He's saddled with a nut
And want to kill me, like he should.

So listen,
Thanks a bunch,
But I'm not getting married.
Go have brunch,
'Cause I'm not getting married.
You've been grand,
But I'm not getting married.
Don't just stand
There, I'm not getting married.
And don't tell Paul,
But I'm not getting married today!

Go. Can't you go?
Why is nobody listening?
Goodbye! Go and cry
At some other person's wake.
If you're quick, for a kick
You could pick up a christening,
But please, on my knees,
There's a human life at stake!

Listen, everybody, I'm afraid you didn't hear,
Or do you want to see a crazy person
Fall apart in front of you?
It isn't only Paul who may be ruining his life, you know,
We'll both of us be losing our identities –
I telephoned my shrink and he said
Maybe I should come and see him Monday,
But by Monday I'll be floating
In the Hudson with the other garbage.

I'm not well,
So I'm not getting married.
You've been swell,
But I'm not getting married.
Clear the hall,
'Cause I'm not getting married.
Thank you all,
But I'm not getting married –
And don't tell Paul,
But I'm not getting married today.

The PRIEST *reappears.*

PRIEST.
Bless this fool, totally insane,
Slipping down the drain,
And bless this day in our hearts –
As it starts to rain…

The PRIEST *disappears.*

PAUL.	JAMIE.
Today is for Jamie.	Go, can't you go?
Jamie,	Look, you know

I give you
The rest of my days,
To cherish

And to keep
You,
To honour you
Forever.
Today is for
Jamie,

My lover,
My partner,

My life,

For the

Rest of my

life.

I adore you all,
But why watch me die?
When I'm only being
    nice?
Look, perhaps
I'll collapse
In the apse
Right before you all,
So take back the cake,
Burn the shoes and boil
    the rice!

Look, I didn't want to
    have to tell you,
But I may be coming
    down with hepatitis
And I'm feeling kind of
    faint,
So if you wanna see me
    faint,
I'll do it happily,
But wouldn't it be
    funnier
To go and watch a
    funeral?
So thank you for the
Twenty-seven dinner
    plates and
Thirty-seven salad
    bowls and
Forty-seven picture
    frames and
Fifty-seven candle
    holders...

PAUL.
    One more thing –

JAMIE.
    I am not getting married!

The PRIEST *and* GUESTS *appear.*

PRIEST *and* GUESTS.
    Amen.

PAUL.
    Softly said:

JAMIE.
    But I'm not getting married!

PRIEST *and* GUESTS.
    Amen.

PAUL.
    With this ring –

JAMIE.
    Still I'm not getting married!

PRIEST *and* GUESTS.
    Amen.

PAUL.
    I thee wed.

JAMIE.
    See, I'm not getting married!

PRIEST *and* GUESTS.
    Amen.

PAUL.	JAMIE.
Let us pray,	Let us pray
And we are	That we're not
Getting married today.	Getting married today!

GROUP.
    Amen!

    BOBBIE *enters.*

PAUL. Jamie?

JAMIE. You're starting!

    PAUL *begins to speak.*

Don't talk, please! Why don't the two of you sit down and talk to each other? I can't think with the two of you following me – everyplace I go – from the bedroom to the bathroom to the kitchen... I feel like I'm leading a parade. Paul, stop staring! I feel it – like bullets – right through my back. No, Paul, please! I'm so crazy I left the refrigerator door open last night, so the orange juice is hot. Here, (*Offering him and* BOBBIE *glasses of orange juice*.) and if you say 'thank you' I will go running right out of this apartment and move into the 'hopeless cases' section at Bellevue Hospital where they'll understand me. Don't talk, please. I apologise, Paul. Oh, Paul, you say whatever you want to say. Whatever you like. Who am *I* telling *you* what to do? Oh, Paul.

Pause.

PAUL. The orange juice is hot. But thanks.

JAMIE. Paul, Jesus! You don't thank a person for hot orange juice!

Smoke rises from the toaster.

The toast! (*Takes two charred pieces of toast out of the toaster.*) Now, I blew the toast.

PAUL. That's okay.

JAMIE. I can't stand it! IT'S NOT OKAY, PAUL. NOTHING ABOUT IT EVEN REMOTELY RESEMBLES OKAY. IT IS THE OPPOSITE OF OKAY. Oh, Bobbie, this is the real me. Crazed!

BOBBIE. I was just thinking that this is probably a much more interesting wedding breakfast than most. And, uh, that one groom certainly has a lot of energy. The other groom is abnormally quiet. And yet a festive atmosphere pervades the room – I guess it's the Maid of Honour, smiling, even as she dies from drinking boiled orange juice.

JAMIE. I would laugh, Bobbie, if it weren't all so tragic. How do I look? Funny?

PAUL. Yeah, that's a funny outfit.

JAMIE. That asshole barber cut my hair like he was on withdrawal. Paul, what are you so happy about all the time?

PAUL. You.

JAMIE. This is the most neurotic... insane... it is... so *crazy* having this enormous wedding and everything after we've been living together all these years! It's embarrassing, Paul. People will think I'm pregnant.

PAUL. That's next year. Listen, if we hurry, we're late.

JAMIE. What am I doing? I'm thirty-one.

PAUL. And perfect.

JAMIE. It's just incredible. Two years with a psychiatrist... and look where it leads. I am just so glad we're not having a Catholic wedding because next year when I get a divorce I won't be a sinner. Whoever would have thought I'd *marry* someone Jewish? Jewish! I mean I didn't even *know* anybody who was Jewish. See, Bobbie. That was probably my main attraction. Look what a little Catholic rebellion will lead to! The very first moment I met Paul, I said to myself, 'That's what I really like... that Jew!' Oh, he was so beautiful... inside and out beautiful. Paul would kiss me and I would think, 'Oh, I've got my very own Jew!'

PAUL. What is all this about me being Jewish today? About three-quarters of your friends are Jewish. Hurry.

JAMIE. Did I ever say I like my friends. I do not. I much prefer my Gentile enemies, at least they leave you alone. And I need to be left alone. I'm just like Bobbie.

BOBBIE. I'm not like that! What are you talking about? Don't answer, we don't have time.

PAUL. Jamie. After all these years, don't you know we match?

JAMIE. The higher you go, the harder you hurt when you fall.

PAUL. I never dropped you yet.

He goes to take a sip of coffee, sees a note in the saucer, then shows the note to BOBBIE. BOBBIE *opens the note.*

BOBBIE. 'Whoever reads this... I love you.' Well, thank you, I love *you*.

JAMIE. Thank him. The phantom. He leaves notes like that all over the place. A person can't stand all that sweetness, Paul. Nobody human can stand all that everlasting affection.

PAUL. Jamie, don't you think we should go?

JAMIE. I can't.

PAUL. Jamie, if anybody should be married, it's you. Tell him, Bobbie.

JAMIE. Bobbie tell me? Who's going to tell Bobbie?

Pause.

BOBBIE. Paul, I am the last person to tell anybody anything like that.

Pause.

PAUL. I see.

BOBBIE. Listen, I'm going to call and say that, ah... that... that we'll be late. That we'll be a little late. The people will be getting there, don't you think? (*Exits.*)

PAUL. Jamie, do you see what you're doing to yourself? Do you know if other people did to you what you do to yourself, they could be put in jail? C'mon.

Sounds of thunder.

JAMIE. Oh, Paul, look... oh, look... it's starting to rain.

BOBBIE *enters with an umbrella.*

BOBBIE. It's starting to rain. Oh, guess who I ran into coming over here today. Tim Kincaid? Remember Tim Kincaid? From school? Well, he's married now. I almost didn't recognise him, all fat and blowsy and...

PAUL. Jamie. C'mon. We're late.

JAMIE. Just because we can doesn't mean we should. I can't do it, Paul. I don't understand how I ever let it get this far.

Sounds of thunder again.

Oh look, will you look at that, now it's really starting to rain… look at it… it's a flood, it's a sign; thank you God, now explain it to him!

PAUL. Jamie, let's go. All our friends are waiting.

JAMIE. That's no reason, Paul. I just can't. I'm so afraid.

PAUL. Of what?

JAMIE. I don't know. I don't know. I just think you're really not for me, Paul. I just think maybe nobody's for me. I never saw one good marriage. Never. Not in my entire life.

PAUL. You just see what you look for, you know. I've seen a lot. It's just fear, Jamie. Married people are no more *marriage* than… oh… musicians are music. Just because some of the people might be wrong – doesn't matter… *it* is still *right*.

JAMIE. Yeah, well, I'll put that on a T-shirt, Paul. (*Looks up; right to* PAUL.) Please. I'm not being emotional. I'm as sane as can be. Paul? I'm sorry. I just don't love you *enough*.

There is a very long pause.

PAUL. Bobbie… would you… call and ah… explain and… I'm… I ah, I… (*Exits.*)

JAMIE. What did I just do?

BOBBIE. You did… what you had to do… I guess… if it was right, you would have gone through with it. That's what I think, anyway. (*Pause.*) Jamie, you know what we should do?

JAMIE. What's that?

BOBBIE. We should get married, us two.

JAMIE. What?

BOBBIE. That would shut them all up. Marry me.

Underscoring: 'Bobbie Baby' music.

JAMIE. Huh?

BOBBIE. You said it before – we're just alike. Why don't we, Jamie?

JAMIE. Why don't we, Bobbie?

COMPANY (*voice-over*).
Bobbie, Bobbie,
Bobbie baby, Bobbie bubi,
Bobbie...

BOBBIE. Marry me! And everybody'll leave us *alone*!

COMPANY (*voice-over*).
Bobbie... Bobbie... how have you been?
Stop by on your way home...
Bobbie, we've been thinking of you...

JAMIE. Isn't this some world? I'm afraid to get married and you're afraid not to. Thank you, Bobbie. I'm really... it's just that you have to want to marry *some*body, not just some*body*.

Sound of thunder again. JAMIE *notices* PAUL*'s umbrella.*

Oh! Christ. He went out without an umbrella or anything. (*Grabs an umbrella for* PAUL.)

He'll get pneumonia. I've got to catch him. I have to get him. I'm getting married. Oh, and he's so good, isn't he? So good. (*Starts to exit.*)

BOBBIE. Jamie!

She throws him the bouquet; JAMIE *catches it and holds it in front of him.*

JAMIE. I'm the next bride. (*Exits.*)

COMPANY (*voice-over*).
Bobbie, come on over for dinner!
We'll be so glad to see you!
Bobbie, come on over for dinner!
Just be the three of us,
Only the three of us,
We loooooove... you!

BOBBIE.

> Marry me a little,
> Love me just enough.
> Cry, but not too often,
> Play, but not too rough.
>
> Keep a tender distance,
> So we'll both be free.
> That's the way it ought to be.
> I'm ready!
>
> Marry me a little,
> Do it with a will.
> Make a few demands
> I'm able to fulfil.
>
> Want me more than others,
> Not exclusively.
> That's the way it ought to be.
> I'm ready!
> I'm ready now!
>
> You can be my best friend.
> I can be your right arm.
> We'll go through a fight or two.
> No harm, no harm.
>
> We'll look not too deep,
> We'll go not too far.
> We won't have to give up a thing,
> We'll stay who we are.
> Right?
>
> Okay, then, I'm ready!
> I'm ready now!
>
> Someone,
> Marry me a little,
> Love me just enough.
> Warm and sweet and easy,
> Just the simple stuff.
>
> Keep a tender distance
> So we'll both be free.

That's the way it ought to be.
I'm ready!

Marry me a little,
Body, heart and soul.
Passionate as hell,
But always in control.
Want me first and foremost,
Keep me company.
That's the way it ought to be.
I'm ready!
I'm ready now!

Oh, how gently we'll talk,
Oh, how softly we'll tread.
All the stings, the ugly things
We'll keep unsaid.

We'll build a cocoon of love and respect.
You promise whatever you like,
I'll never collect.
Right?

Okay, then, I'm ready!
I'm ready now!
Someone...
I'm ready! I'm ready! I'm ready!
I'm... I'm...

COUPLES (*voice-over*).
Bobbie, Bobbie,
Bobbie baby, Bobbie bubi,
Bobbie...

Bobbie, Bobbie,
Bobbie baby, Bobbie bubi,
Bobbie...

Lights come up on all the birthday guests looking at
BOBBIE *as in Act One, Scene One.* BOBBIE *stares at them*
as they blow out the candles.

Curtain.

ACT TWO

Scene One

BOBBIE*'s apartment.*

FIVE COUPLES.
> Bobbie, Bobbie,
> Ba ba ba ba ba ba ba ba…
> Bobbie, Bobbie,
> Ba ba ba ba ba ba ba ba…
> Bobbie…

Lights come up on the birthday party with BOBBIE *about to blow out the candles and all five* COUPLES *standing around her.*

JAMIE. Well, our blessings, Bobbie.

JENNY. Don't tell your wish, Bobbie, or it won't come true.

BOBBIE *tries to blow out the candles but most of them remain lit. The others blow out the rest.*

JOANNE. You just blew it.

JAMIE. It probably was a wish you wouldn't have got anyway, Bobbie.

DAVID. You wish for a husband, Bobbie?

PETER. Don't. Hang in there.

SARAH. Stay exactly the same. You may be the one constant in this world of variables.

HARRY. I don't know, Sarah, you can't stay in your thirties forever.

JENNY. You'll still get your wish, Bobbie.

JOANNE. Won't.

PAUL. I think she still gets her wish.

JOANNE. I say she won't.

LARRY. Joanne, come on. (*To the others*.) See, when she and Bobbie get together –

JOANNE. I know the goddam rules for birthday candle blowing out, Larry. I've had enough for a wax museum. And I'm telling you, if you do not blow out all the candles on the cake, you do not get your wish.

BOBBIE. All right, all right! Actually, I didn't wish for anything.

DAVID. What do you mean you didn't wish for...

PETER. Come on, tell, everybody's so curious.

SUSAN. Tell, but lie.

BOBBIE. Thank you for including me in your thoughts, your lives.

All the other characters exit on their following lines, leaving BOBBIE *alone*.

PAUL. Stay exactly as you are, Bobbie.

SARAH. That's right, you perfect person.

SUSAN. You stay exactly as you are.

Underscoring: 'Bobbie Baby' music.

JOANNE. Everyone adores you. What an awful thing.

LARRY. I'd kiss you goodnight, Bobbie, but Joanne gets jealous.

JAMIE. Things always happen for the best... I don't even believe that myself.

BOBBIE. I mean, when you've got friends like mine...

'Side by Side by Side' introduction starts.

(*Softly*.) I mean, when you've got friends like mine...

(*Sings*.)
   Isn't it warm,
   Isn't it rosy,
   Side by side –

SARAH. She's such a treasure.

BOBBIE.
> – by side?

SARAH. Isn't she a treasure?

BOBBIE.
> Ports in a storm,
> Comfy and cozy,
> Side by side –

PETER. She never loses her cool.

BOBBIE.
> – by side?

HARRY. I envy that.

BOBBIE.
> Everything shines.
> How sweet –

BOBBIE, JENNY *and* DAVID.
> Side by side –

SUSAN. We're just so fond of her.

BOBBIE.
> – by side.
> Parallel lines
> Who meet –

HARRY, SARAH, JAMIE, PAUL, SUSAN *and* PETER.
> Love her –
> Can't get enough of her.

BOBBIE.
> Everyone winks,
> Nobody's nosy,
> Side by side –

JOANNE. She feels exactly the way I do –

BOBBIE.
> – by side.

JOANNE.
– about everything.

BOBBIE.
You make the drinks
And I'll bring the posy.
Side by side –

LARRY. She's always there when you need her.

BOBBIE.
– by side.

PAUL. That's class.

BOBBIE.
One is lonely and two is boring,
Think what you can keep ignoring.
Side –

JAMIE. She's my best friend.

PAUL *looks at him.*

BOBBIE.
– by side –

JAMIE (*touching* PAUL). Second best.

BOBBIE.
– by side.

COUPLES.
Pal and pinch-hitter,
Plus a perfect babysitter!

Year after year,
Older and older –

SUSAN. It's amazing. We've gotten older every year and she
seems to stay exactly the same.

COUPLES.
Sharing a tear,
Lending a shoulder –

PAUL. You know what comes to my mind when I see her? The Chrysler Building. Isn't that weird?

COUPLES.
> Always in fun,
> No strain –

JOANNE. Sometimes I catch her looking and looking. I just look right back.

COUPLES.
> Permanent sun,
> No rain.
> We're so crazy, she's so sane.
> Everyone blends,
> Like a good whiskey –

DAVID. A person like Bobbie doesn't have the good things and she doesn't have the bad things. But she doesn't have the good things.

COUPLES.
> Intimate friends,
> But nothing that's risky –

HARRY. Let me make her a drink. She's the only person I know, I feel should drink more.

BOBBIE.
> One's impossible, two is dreary,
> Three is company, safe and cheery,
> Side –

SARAH. She always looks like she's keeping score.

BOBBIE.
> By side –

SARAH. Who's winning, Bobbie?

BOBBIE.
> Here is the church,
> Here is the steeple,
> Open the doors and
> See all the crazy, married people!

The scene becomes an exuberant birthday party.

COUPLES.
>What would we do without you?
>How would we ever get through?
>Who would I complain to for hours?
>Who'd bring me the flowers
>When I have the flu?
>
>Who'd finish yesterday's stew?
>Who'd take the kids to the zoo?
>Who is so cool?
>And who is so deep?
>And who would keep him/her company
>When I want to sleep?
>How would we ever get through?
>What would we do without you?

Dance break, which leaves them out of breath.

>Huff. Huff. Huff. Huff.
>
>What would we do without you?
>How would we ever get through?
>Should there be some marital tension,
>It's your intervention
>Begins us anew.
>
>Who could we open up to,
>Secrets we keep from guess-who?
>Who is so safe and who is so sound?
>You never need an analyst with Bobbie around.
>How could we ever get through?
>What would we do without you?

Dance break.

BOBBIE.
>Huff. Huff. Huff. Huff. (*Throws up in a bucket.*)
>Bleaahhh…

COUPLES.
>What would we do without you?
>How would we ever get through?
>Who sends anniversary wishes?
>Who helps with the dishes
>And never says boo?

Who changes subjects on cue?
Who cheers us up when we're blue?

Who is a flirt but never a threat,
Reminds us of our birthdays which we always forget?
How would we ever get through?
What would we do without you?

Huff. Huff. Huff. Huff.

What would we do without you?
How would we ever get...
How would we ever get...
How would we ever get...
How would we ever get... through?
What would we do without you?

BOBBIE.
    Just what you usually do!

COUPLES.
    Right!
    You who sit with us...
    You who share with us...
    You who fit with us...
    You who bear with us...
    Yoo-hoo! Yoo-hoo!
    Yoo-hoo! Yoo-hoo!

BOBBIE.
    Okay, now everybody – !

ALL.
    Isn't it warm,
    Isn't it rosy,
    Side by side?

JAMIE *and* PAUL *and* SUSAN *and* PETER *each do a brief dance break together.*

    Ports in a storm,
    Comfy and cozy,
    Side by side?

JENNY *and* DAVID *and* SARAH *and* HARRY *each do a brief dance break together.*

Everything shines,
How sweet,
Side by side.

JOANNE *and* LARRY *do a brief dance break together.*

Parallel lines
Who meet,
Side by side.

BOBBIE *attempts a brief dance break on her own. Nobody joins her.*

ALL (*except* BOBBIE).
Year after year, older and older,
Side by side.
Sharing a tear and lending a shoulder,
Side by side.
Two's impossible, two is gloomy,
Give another number to me,
Side by side, by side,

By side, by side, by side, by side, by side,
By side, by side, by side, by side, by side –

By side!

All COUPLES *exit, leaving* BOBBIE *alone onstage.*

Scene Two

BOBBIE*'s apartment*. ANDY *enters wearing his flight attendant's uniform.*

ANDY. Oh! It's a gorgeous apartment.

BOBBIE. Thank you.

ANDY. Just gorgeous. Did you do it yourself?

BOBBIE. Yes, I did, yes.

ANDY. Yourself?

BOBBIE.... Yes.

ANDY. Really?

BOBBIE. Really.

ANDY. Well, it's gorgeous. Did you really do it all yourself?

BOBBIE. Yes! Why? Did you hear that I didn't?

ANDY. No. (*Opens the bedroom door.*) Wow. Isn't that tasteful and interesting?

BOBBIE. Yes. I'll take it. I mean I've always liked my apartment but I'm never really in it. I just seem to pass through it on my way to the bedroom. (*Goes into the bedroom.*)

ANDY. Oh, it's beautifully laid out. (*Doing the flight-attendant's two-finger wave forward and back as he demonstrates.*) See how nicely all the furniture is placed into areas to make it so warm and sweet and tucked in.

BOBBIE. How about that?

ANDY. And the choice of colours is so relaxing and simple and feminine.

BOBBIE. Uh-huh.

ANDY. You never really spend any time in here? And it's so great. But maybe that's why you like it so much. If you don't spend much time in it, it makes it special.

BOBBIE. Yes. And this is the bedroom over here.

He crosses to it.

You love it, I can tell. Well, I can always look for another place.

BOBBIE *and* ANDY *start to make out.*

SARAH *and* HARRY *enter.*

HARRY.
    Sarah –

SARAH.
    Yes?

HARRY.
    Bobbie –

SARAH.
    What?

HARRY.
    I worry –

SARAH.
    Why?

HARRY.
    She's all alone.

SARAH.
    Mm.

HARRY.
    There's no one –

SARAH.
    Where?

HARRY.
    In her life.

SARAH.
    Oh.

HARRY.

Bobbie ought to have a fella.

Poor baby, all alone,
Nothing much to do except to check her phone.
We're the only closeness that she's really known.
Poor baby…

JENNY *and* DAVID *enter*.

DAVID.

Honey –

JENNY.

Yes?

DAVID.

Bobbie –

JENNY.

What?

DAVID.

I worry.

JENNY.

Why?

DAVID.

It's such a waste.

JENNY.

Mm.

DAVID.

There's no one.

JENNY.

Where?

DAVID.

In her life.

JENNY.

Oh.

DAVID.

> Bobbie ought to have a fella.

> Poor baby –
> So unfair,
> Nothing left to do except to wash her hair.
> Maybe I should call her, just to –

JENNY.

> Don't go there…

DAVID.

> Poor baby…

ANDY. Right after I became a flight attendant, a friend of mine who had a garden apartment gave me a cocoon for my bedroom. She collects things like that, insects and caterpillars and stuff… It was attached to a twig and she said one morning I'd wake up to a beautiful butterfly in my bedroom – when it hatched. She told me that when they come out they're soaking wet and there is a drop of blood there, too – isn't that fascinating – but within an hour they dry off and then they begin to fly. Well, I told her I had a cat. I had a cat then, but she said just put the cocoon somewhere where the cat couldn't get at it… which is impossible, but what can you do? So I put it up high on a ledge where the cat never went, and the next morning it was still there, at least so it seemed safe to leave it. Well, anyway, almost a week later very, very early this one morning the girl calls me, and she said, 'Andy, do you have a butterfly this morning?' I told her to hold on and managed to get up and look and there on that ledge I saw this wet spot and a little speck of blood but no butterfly, and I thought 'Oh dear God in heaven, the cat got it.' I picked up the phone to tell this girl and just then suddenly I spotted it under the table, it was moving one wing. The cat had got at it, but it was still alive. So I told the girl and she got so upset and she said 'Oh no – oh, God, no – don't you see that's a life – a living thing?' Well, I got dressed and took it to the park and put it on a rose, it was summer then, and it looked like it was going to be all right – I think, anyway. But that girl – I really felt damaged by her – awful – that was just cruel. I got home and called her back and said, 'Listen, I'm a living thing too, you shithead!' (*Pause.*) I never saw her again.

Pause.

BOBBIE. That reminds me of something I did… in Miami…
I mean it's not exactly the same but in a way. Well, you'll
see. I met a guy, a handsome guy, at a party one night and,
well, it was like you and me. We just – connected. You don't
mind my telling you this, do you?

ANDY. No.

BOBBIE. It just… came to my mind. Anyway, we just
connected, in such a beautiful way… exactly like tonight.
Except we couldn't even contain ourselves. It was incredible.
We were talking and suddenly we realised we just couldn't talk
anymore. No sounds came. We stood looking at each other and
we were both bathed in perspiration. Our breathing was so
short and our legs were trembling and we just left. We drove to
one of those strips there where they have all those motels, and
we didn't even say anything. We got inside that room and we
started touching and kissing and laughing and holding and it
was all going to be over too quickly, so I said I should go get
lots of Champagne and some massage oil and we should get
beautifully smashed and start rubbing… well, you know.

He was in no condition to drive, so I rushed out of there and
I drove around until I could find a liquor store and a drugstore
open and I got all this Champagne and the oil and finally
I started back to the motel and – I – could not – find – it.

I looked for over three hours. I never found it. And I never
saw him again either.

ANDY. Huhh. That's the most incredible story I have ever heard.

BOBBIE *helps him out of his jacket.*

You poor poor girl. And you drove around for three hours?

BOBBIE *unbuttons* ANDY*'s shirt and begins undressing
him.*

BOBBIE. More! All night I tried to find that motel. I mean all
night. With the oil and all that Champagne and my hands
trembling and sweat running down my face.

ANDY. That is so sad! I just don't know what to do.

BOBBIE. I know.

On the bed kissing; suddenly ANDY *stops and sits up.*

ANDY. But wait a minute. Those stories don't really follow.
I don't see the connection. Unless... oh... you see yourself
as the wounded butterfly.

BOBBIE *looks up to the sky with a 'thank you' expression.*

BOBBIE. Yes! That's it!

They go under the covers.

HARRY *and* DAVID *enter.*

HARRY.
    Bobbie...

DAVID.
    Bobbie...

HARRY.
    Bobbie, sweetheart...

DAVID.
    Bobbie, baby...

The following sections overlap.

HARRY.
    You know, no one
    Wants you to be happy
    More than I do,
    No one, but
    Isn't he a little bit, well,
    You know – ?
    Face it.
    Why him?
    Better no one.
    Isn't he a little bit, well,
    You know – ?
    Face it.
    Why these meaningless relationships?
    They can't make you happy.
    But you know better.

DAVID.

>You know, no one
>Wants you to be happy
>More than I do.
>No one, but –
>Isn't he a little bit, well
>You know – ?
>Face it.
>Why him?
>Better no one.
>Isn't he a little bit –
>Well, you know better.

PAUL *enters*.

PAUL.

>You know, no one
>Wants you to be happy
>More than I do.
>No one, but
>Isn't he a little bit –
>Well, you know?
>Face it.

PETER *enters*.

PETER.

>Why these meaningless relationships?
>They can't make you happy.
>But you know better.

LARRY *enters*.

LARRY.

>You know, no one
>Wants you to be happy
>More than I do.
>No one, but –

ALL MEN.

>Isn't he a little bit, well – ?

The following lines overlap.

HARRY.
Dumb…

PAUL.
Lightweight…

PETER.
Bloodless…

DAVID.
Sly…

LARRY.
Young?

PETER.
Too toothy…
Too happy,
Don't trust him, and…

PAUL.
Too eager…
A bit too smooth…
And immature.

HARRY.
Where is he from?
He's kind of weird…

DAVID.
Uncouth…
Disturbed and…

LARRY.
He's young enough to be your son –
Correction, *grandson*…

ALL MEN.
Poor baby,
All alone.
Throw a lonely dog a bone,
It's still a bone.
We're the only comfort that she's really known.
Poor baby.

'Tick-Tock': a sequence in which BOBBIE *sees various versions of her future self, a nightmarish dream that depicts her with partners and children.*

Lights come up on the bedroom as before. The alarm goes off. Music starts as ANDY *gets up and begins dressing.* BOBBIE, *just waking up, sees this and sleepily sings:*

BOBBIE.
     Where you going?

ANDY.
     Barcelona.

BOBBIE.
     …Oh…

ANDY.
     Don't get up.

BOBBIE.
     Do you have to?

ANDY.
     Yes, I have to.

BOBBIE.
     …Oh…

ANDY.
     Don't get up.

     Pause.

     Now you're angry.

BOBBIE.
     No, I'm not.

ANDY.
     Yes, you are.

BOBBIE.
     No, I'm not.
     Put your things down.

ANDY.
> See, you're angry.

BOBBIE.
> No, I'm not.

ANDY.
> Yes, you are.

BOBBIE.
> No, I'm not.
> Put your wings down
> And stay.

ANDY.
> I'm leaving.

BOBBIE.
> Why?

ANDY.
> To go to –

BOBBIE.
> Stay.

ANDY.
> I have to –

BOTH.
> Fly –

BOBBIE.
> I know,

BOTH.
> To Barcelona.

BOBBIE.
> Look,
> You're a very special guy,
> Not just an overnight.

Yawning.

> No, you're a very special guy.
> And not because you're bright –

Not *just* because you're bright.
You're just a very special guy, Randy!

ANDY.
Andy...

BOBBIE.
Andy...

Pause.

ANDY.
Thank you.

Pause.

BOBBIE.
Whatcha thinking?

ANDY.
Barcelona.

BOBBIE.
...Oh...

ANDY.
Flight 18.

BOBBIE.
Stay a minute.

ANDY.
I would like to.

BOBBIE.
So – ?

ANDY.
Don't be mean.

BOBBIE.
Stay a minute.

ANDY.
No, I can't.

BOBBIE.
Yes, you can.

ANDY.
No, I can't.

BOBBIE.
> Where you going?

ANDY.
> Barcelona.

BOBBIE.
> So you said.

ANDY.
> And Madrid.

BOBBIE.
> Bon voyage.

ANDY.
> On a Boeing.

BOBBIE.
> Goodnight.

ANDY.
> You're angry.

BOBBIE.
> No.

ANDY.
> I've got to –

BOBBIE.
> Right.

ANDY.
> Report to –

BOBBIE.
> Go.

ANDY.
> That's not to
> Say
> That if I had my way…
> Oh well, I guess, okay.

BOBBIE.
> What?

ANDY.

I'll stay.

He jumps back into bed.

BOBBIE.

But…

Oh, God.

Scene Three

SUSAN *and* PETER*'s apartment.* SUSAN *and* BOBBIE *are on the terrace again.*

SUSAN. Yeah… we fixed it up… took care of lots of things. Planted. Nice. We really worked hard. Now we practically live out here.

BOBBIE. The terrace is great. The dinner was great. Thank you.

SUSAN. Isn't Peter a great cook.

BOBBIE. It's none of my business, but is everything okay again? I mean, you both seem so happy.

SUSAN. Oh, yeah. We've both changed so much – really grown. I mean it's like the pressure is off, you see… I don't feel so tied down or strangled or caught anymore. And we really talk now. I mean we were miserable for so long. Now it's fine… like… oh, really being free again.

BOBBIE. Terrific. Great. I'm so happy for you both.

SUSAN. It's hell getting a divorce in New York you know. Forget it. We gave up. It's like they think up everything to keep you married. Plus for instance, where was Peter going to find an apartment if he moved out? And when he finally did find one, the building owner wanted the first two months' and last month security plus a finder's fee, plus money under the table, plus the rental agency fee, and the super wanted money for letting him in, and the tenants wanted money for moving out and he finally told them all to go screw themselves. Besides which, he insisted I keep at least half of everything... no matter what. If it was up to Peter he would have cut the carpet in half so we'd have two runners! He was fantastic – involved and nicer, so... giving – I don't know – better! It all got better. Plus the courts here are so crowded... everybody's getting a divorce.

BOBBIE. Remember last year when everybody was getting married?

PETER (*entering*). The kids are in bed.

BOBBIE. Peter, I just said to Susan I'm so glad you didn't get that divorce.

PETER. What?

SUSAN. No. That's what I was just saying, Bobbie. We flew out to Nevada and got the divorce.

PETER. It's beautiful down there.

BOBBIE. Oh... oh...

Oh...

So you're not married now?

SUSAN. Married? We tried that. No. Divorce is better for us. We might get divorced again.

PETER. The truth is we never should have married – we should have just divorced right away. We're terrific divorced.

SUSAN. I think we were always just meant to be divorced.

BOBBIE. Huh! Well, still it takes two to make a happy divorce. And, God knows it's working. And I think you're terrific together.

PETER. So do I.

SUSAN. So do I.

SUSAN *touches her stomach, showing* BOBBIE *that she is pregnant again – early stages*.

BOBBIE. Wow.

Scene Four

The stage is alive with the activity of a nightclub. JOANNE *is watching* BOBBIE *and* LARRY *dancing with the* PATRONS. BOBBIE *returns to the table.* LARRY *keeps dancing. Dance music softens.* JOANNE *and* BOBBIE *grow increasingly drunk as the scene progresses.* LARRY *remains quite sober.*

BOBBIE. I think they're going to hurt themselves.

JOANNE. What if their mothers came in and saw them doing that. Think of their poor mothers. He's embarrassing.

(*Yelling in* LARRY*'s direction.*) Think of your poor mother!

BOBBIE. He's not what you'd call self-conscious.

JOANNE. He's not what you'd call! Big show-off. It really shocks me to see a grown man dance like that! I am shocked, you hear, shocked! Where was I? Oh – my first husband. He is so difficult to remember. Even when you're with him. We got married here in New York. I was just out of college. See. He was here on some business deal, but he owned a big meat-packing company in Chicago. Attractive? Well, we lived in New York for almost a year and then one day he had to go back to Chicago. And you know, he was actually surprised when I told him I would just wait here for him. I mean, I still really don't know quite where Chicago is. It's over there somewhere. (*Points front.*) He used to call me every night. For months we would both be sitting on the phone long distance, just breathing at each other. After a while – what more is there to say?

Pause.

BOBBIE. The phone is a phenomenon. Really. The best way for two people to be connected and detached at the same time.

JOANNE. Second only to marriage. Anyway, he said he didn't really plan to come back... so I knew we were in a tiny dilemma – or at least he was. I was still too young. But I was old enough to know where I was living, and I had no intention of leaving New York. I have never left New York. Never have, never will. And least of all would I ever want to go to a place where they actually feel honoured being called 'hog butchers to the world'. They're proud of that! I said, 'Kiss off, Rodney,' but I said it nicer. Well, we got a divorce. A divorce. Huh – ! One word means all of that. (*Calling to a passing* WAITER.) Another drink… sir. OH, SIR!

The WAITER *ignores her. The dance ends;* LARRY *returns to* JOANNE *and* BOBBIE.

LARRY. Whew!

JOANNE (*looking up at him and then to* BOBBIE). The eagle has landed.

LARRY. You all had a few while I was dancing, huh?

JOANNE. Larry, what the hell was all that carrying on? What was that? Shocking.

LARRY. I asked you to dance.

JOANNE. I don't think standing bumping around and making an ass out of oneself is a dance. I find it unbelievably humiliating watching my own husband flouncing around the dance floor, jerking all over the place like Ann Miller. Take off the red shoes, Larry. Off.

LARRY (*to* BOBBIE). Was I that good?

BOBBIE. Amazingly good.

JOANNE. Just sit there and catch your breath – or whatever you chorus boys do.

LARRY. Joanne, I love it when you're jealous. Kiss me.

JOANNE. I hated dinner. I hated the opera, and I hate it here. What I need is more to drink – and look at Bobbie, how desperately she needs another drink.

The WAITER *enters again.*

SIR. SIR! SIR, SIR! Better get your identification out, Larry. TWO MORE BOURBONS AND A VODKA STINGER! SIR! Do you know that I am suddenly at an age where I find myself too old for the young ones and too young for the old people. I'm nowhere. I think I better drink to me. To me – the generation gap. (*Yells at the other* PATRONS *in the club.*) I AM THE GENERATION GAP! (*To* LARRY *and* BOBBIE.)

Are they staring at me? Let 'em stare – let 'em. This whole country is about young. And it's about money. And if you ain't got one you sure better have the other. (*To the other* PATRONS.) STOP STARING!

LARRY. What time is it?

JOANNE. In real life? Will somebody get us another drink!

Just then, the WAITER *delivers them.*

Oh, you did. So aggressive.

She picks up her drink.

I'd like to propose a toast.

Here's to the ladies who lunch...
Everybody laugh.
Lounging in their caftans and planning a brunch
On their own behalf.
Off to the gym,
Then to a fitting,
Claiming they're fat.
And looking grim
'Cause they've been sitting
Choosing a hat –
Does anyone still wear a hat?
I'll drink to that.

Drinks.

Here's to the girls who stay smart –
Aren't they a gas?
Rushing to their classes in digital art,
Wishing it would pass.
Another long exhausting day,
Another thousand dollars,
A matinee, a Pinter play,
Perhaps a piece of Mahler's –
I'll drink to that.

Drinks.

And one for Mahler.

Drinks again.

> Here's to the girls in their prime –
> Aren't they too much?
> Keeping house but clutching a copy of *Time*
> Just to keep in touch.
>
> The ones who follow the rules,
> And meet themselves at the schools,
> Too busy to know that they're fools –
> Aren't they a gem?
> I'll drink to them.
> Let's all drink to them!
>
> And here's to the girls who just watch –
> Aren't they the best?
> When they get depressed, it's a bottle of Scotch
> Plus a little jest.
> Another chance to disapprove,
> Another brilliant zinger,
> Another reason not to move,
> Another vodka stinger –
> (*Screams.*) Aaaahh – (*Back to normal.*) I'll drink to that.

Drinks.

> So here's to the girls on the go –
> Everybody tries.
> Look into their eyes and you'll see what they know:
> Everybody dies.
>
> A toast to that invincible bunch,
> The dinosaurs surviving the crunch –
> Let's hear it for the ladies who lunch!
> Everybody rise! Rise!
> Rise! Rise! Rise! Rise! Rise! Rise!
> Rise!

The lights come back up on the nightclub. It has emptied.

I would like a cigarette, Larry. Remember when everyone used to smoke? How it was more – uh – festive… happier or something. Now every place is not unlike an operating room, for Chrissake.

A WAITER *tries to intercept* JOANNE *smoking.* LARRY *waves him away, indicating he'll deal with it.*

BOBBIE. I never smoked.

JOANNE. Why?

BOBBIE. I don't know. I meant to. Does that count?

JOANNE. Meant to! Meant to! Story of your life. Meant to! Jesus, baby, you are lifted right out of some case history. You're always outside, knocking at the door while everybody is inside dancing at the party. Now I insist you smoke. I'm pulling you through a door right now. Your first compromise. (*Rips open a pack of cigarettes and holds it in front of her.*) Here, Bobbie! Smoke!

BOBBIE. No, thank you.

LARRY. Joanne, honey, c'mon – she doesn't.

BOBBIE. You smoke. I'll watch.

JOANNE. Watch? Did you hear yourself? Huh? Hear what you just said, kiddo? Watch. I am offering you a chance to…

BOBBIE (*interrupting*). I don't want one.

JOANNE. Because you're weak… I hate people who are weak! (*Lights a cigarette, inhales deeply, exhales.*) That's the best. Better than Prozac. Smoking may be the only thing that separates us from the lower forms.

LARRY. You wanna split?

JOANNE. Of what?

LARRY (*to* BOBBIE). See, every day Joanne tests me to see if I'll go away. Twice a year my wife here packs up to leave so I'll ask her to stay. My mother was a very difficult woman… and my old man left her… and he regretted it until the day he died. Now me, hey, I married this imperious broad who's got no self-esteem. This lady who hears a bell and charges in the ring so nobody will see what a pushover she is. I've got a wife who still has a hard time believing that she found a guy she daily fascinates. And, unlike my father, I'm a very happy man. She doesn't act like this when you're not around, Bobbie.

I hope you get to meet Joanne sometime. She's really a terrific lady. In fact, if you ever decide to get married, Bobbie –

JOANNE. Don't ever get married, Bobbie. Never. Why should you?

BOBBIE. Oh, for company, I don't know. Like everybody else.

JOANNE. Who else?

BOBBIE. Everybody that ever fell in love and got married.

JOANNE. I know both couples and they're both divorced. Oh, Larry, you interrupted me before. See what happens when you rush me. I wanted to toast my second husband.

LARRY (*getting up*). It's late. I'm going to the john. And when I come back we'll be leaving. The holiday is ending. Okay? (*Exits.*)

BOBBIE (*calling off to* LARRY). I got the check. He's off to pay the check.

JOANNE *stares unmovingly at* BOBBIE.

Or maybe buy the place. I do like to pay, some of the time. (*Pause.*) You have a good third husband, Joanne. He's a good man. Anyway, thank you for the evening. I'm glad I joined you. I was really feeling low... really depressed. I drank, but you really put it away tonight. The last several times you and I have gotten together, I've had shameful hangovers... abominable. We may be doing permanent damage – think of that? We have good times and it's a blast, yes? Whatever you say! (*Pause.*) No. I don't care for a cigarette if that is what you're trying to stare me into. I am a product of my generation and I do not smoke. My age group is a very uptight age group. Whew! It's drunk out tonight. What are you looking at, Joanne? It's my charisma, huh? Well, stop looking at my charisma!

JOANNE (*still staring*). You know what I think? I think you and Larry should make it.

Pause.

BOBBIE. I beg your pardon?

JOANNE. I think you and Larry should make it.

BOBBIE. Make what?

JOANNE. There's our place. It's free tomorrow after two. I'll be at the gym. Don't talk. Don't do your teenage folksy Doris Day with me. You're a terribly attractive woman. The kind of woman most men want. I'm opening another door for you, Bobbie. Larry will take care of you.

BOBBIE. But who would I take care of?

JOANNE. Well, did you hear yourself? Did you hear what you just said, kiddo?

BOBBIE. I didn't mean it like that.

JOANNE. Oh, I just heard a door open.

BOBBIE (*after a beat*). You think... I haven't looked at all that? Commitment and marriages and all that? What do you get for it? You've said it yourself, over and over. What do you get?

LARRY (*re-enters*). Well, the check is paid and... (*Looks at the emotional* BOBBIE.) What's wrong?

BOBBIE. You think I haven't looked at that, marriages and all that. What do you get for it? What do you get?

LARRY. What's happened?

JOANNE. I just did someone a big favour. C'mon, Larry, let's go home.

She gets up, unsteady on her feet. Underscoring: 'Bobbie Baby' music.

BOBBIE (*as they depart*). What do you get?!

LARRY (*to* JOANNE). Lean on me. I'll hold you.

JOANNE *does*.

JOANNE. Of course you will.

The COUPLES *enter and stand scattered around* BOBBIE. *As they sing, their voices overlap.*

DAVID.
    Bobbie…

JENNY.
    Bobbie…

PAUL.
    Bobbie baby…

PETER.
    Bobbie honey…

SUSAN.
    Boo boo…

SARAH.
    Bobbie darling…

HARRY.
    Bobbie, we've been trying to call you.

JAMIE.
    Bobbie…

LARRY.
    Bobbie…

PAUL.
    Bobbie sugar…

JENNY.
    Bobbie sweetie…

SARAH.
    Angel, I've got something to tell you.

SUSAN.
    Sweetheart…

JOANNE.
    Kiddo…

HARRY.
    Bobbie, love…

PETER.
    Bobbie, honey…

JAMIE *and* PAUL.
> Bobbie, we've been trying to reach you all day.

LARRY.
> Bobbie...

HARRY.
> Bobbie...

DAVID.
> Bobbie baby...

HARRY.
> Bobbie...

SUSAN.
> Bobbie...

DAVID *and* JENNY.
> The kids were asking, Bobbie...

PETER.
> Honey...

JOANNE.
> Kiddo...

LARRY *and* JOANNE.
> Bobbie, there was something we wanted to say.

SARAH *and* HARRY.
> Bobbie...

PAUL.
> Bobbie baby...

PETER.
> What have you been up to, honey?

DAVID *and* JENNY.
> We left a message.

COUPLES.
> Bobbie...

BOBBIE.
> STOP!

A pause. They all freeze.

What do you get?

Someone to hold you too close,
Someone to hurt you too deep,
Someone to sit in your chair,
To ruin your sleep...

PAUL. That's true, but there's more than that.

SARAH. Is that all you think there is to it?

HARRY. You've got so many reasons for *not* being with
someone, but Bobbie, you haven't got one good reason for
being alone.

LARRY. Come on. You're on to something, Bobbie. You're on
to something.

BOBBIE.
Someone to need you too much,
Someone to know you too well,
Someone to pull you up short,
To put you through hell...

JENNY. You see what you look for, you know.

JOANNE. You're not a kid anymore, Bobbie. I don't think
you'll ever be a kid again, kiddo.

PETER. Hey, buddy. Don't be afraid that it won't be perfect...
the only thing to be afraid of really is that it won't *be*!

DAVID. Don't stop now! Keep going!

BOBBIE.
Someone you have to let in.
Someone whose feelings you spare,
Someone who, like it or not, will want you to share
A little, a lot...

PETER. And what does all that mean?

LARRY. Bobbie, how do you know so much about it when
you've never been there?

HARRY. It's much better living it than looking at it, Bobbie.

SUSAN. Add them up, Bobbie. Add them up.

Everyone exits, leaving BOBBIE *alone.*

BOBBIE.
>Someone to crowd you with love,
>Someone to force you to care,
>Someone to make you come through
>Who'll always be there,
>As frightened as you,
>Of being alive,
>Being alive, being alive, being alive.

JAMIE *re-enters.*

JAMIE. Blow out the candles, Bobbie, and make a wish. *Want* something! Want *something*!

JAMIE *exits.*

BOBBIE.
>Somebody hold me too close,
>Somebody hurt me too deep,
>Somebody sit in my chair
>And ruin my sleep
>And make me aware
>Of being alive, being alive.
>
>Somebody need me too much,
>Somebody know me too well,
>Somebody pull me up short
>And put me through hell
>And give me support
>For being alive.
>Make me alive,
>Make me alive.
>
>Make me confused,
>Mock me with praise,
>Let me be used,
>Vary my days.
>But alone is alone, not alive.
>
>Somebody crowd me with love,
>Somebody force me to care,
>Somebody let me come through,
>I'll always be there

As frightened as you,
To help us survive
Being alive, being alive, being alive.

Scene Five

BOBBIE*'s apartment. The* COMPANY *are all waiting for*
BOBBIE.

COUPLES.
　　Bobbie, Bobbie,
　　Ba ba ba ba ba ba ba ba...
　　Bobbie, Bobbie...
　　Ba ba ba ba ba ba ba ba...
　　Bobbie.

*We hear footsteps in the distance growing louder. The lights
are turned down; a key is heard in a lock, but it is another
door in the building that opens and closes. Pause.*

LARRY. Must have been the apartment across the hall.

　　Pause.

HARRY. This is the craziest thing... huh?

JAMIE. Do you think something's wrong?

PAUL (*after a brief pause*). No. I think something's right.

JAMIE. So do I.

SUSAN. Maybe she forgot.

SARAH. How can anyone forget a surprise birthday?

JOANNE. Or... maybe the surprise is on us. I think I got the
　　message. C'mon, Larry, let's go home.

LARRY. Yeah, I think we should.

PAUL. Yes, I think we can go now.

SARAH. Maybe we should leave her a note.

HARRY. Maybe we should leave her alone.

SUSAN. I'll call her tomorrow.

PETER. Don't.

SUSAN. I won't.

DAVID. Jenny?

JENNY. What?

DAVID. Nothing.

JOANNE. Okay. All together, everybody.

ALL. Happy birthday, Bobbie.

They exit the apartment, leaving it empty. From out of the shadows steps BOBBIE. *She enters the apartment, grabs the '35' helium balloons and pops them with a knife. She then picks up a fire extinguisher and sets it off at the candles. One candle remains lit. She smiles, leans forward and blows out the final candle.*

Curtain.